DIGITAL MEDIA
Unravelling the Hype

Gurleen Kaur Wadhwa

BLUEROSE PUBLISHERS
India | U.K.

Copyright © Gurleen Kaur Wadhwa 2024

All rights reserved by author. No part of this publication may be reproduced, stored in a retrieval system or transmitted in any form or by any means, electronic, mechanical, photocopying, recording or otherwise, without the prior permission of the author. Although every precaution has been taken to verify the accuracy of the information contained herein, the publisher assume no responsibility for any errors or omissions. No liability is assumed for damages that may result from the use of information contained within.

BlueRose Publishers takes no responsibility for any damages, losses, or liabilities that may arise from the use or misuse of the information, products, or services provided in this publication.

For permissions requests or inquiries regarding this publication, please contact:

BLUEROSE PUBLISHERS
www.BlueRoseONE.com
info@bluerosepublishers.com
+91 8882 898 898
+4407342408967

ISBN: 978-93-6783-775-7

Cover Design & Editing: Sam V. Rao
Typesetting: Tanya Raj Upadhyay

First Edition: December 2024

Dedicated to

My husband, Himank Wadhwa

My son Naprajit Wadhwa and

My daughter Krisha Wadhwa

ACKNOWLEDGEMENTS

Acknowledgement is never the full expression of one's gratitude to the numerous people whose timely and helpful hints and suggestions is what made the production of this book possible. I would like to express my wholehearted and sincere thanks especially to my husband without whose cooperation and patience I would not have been able to complete this book. I would also like to express my sincere appreciation to a senior faculty and friend, whose input and suggestions, many of which were very practical and helpful, were duly incorporated into this book, and have helped raise the standard of this book.

I am also thankful to BlueRose Publications. who kindly agreed to the publication of this book and who promised to be of assistance in any further books that I might publish under their banner in the future.

FOREWORD

Digital Media, as you all are very well aware, has made its presence felt, only too keenly, in every sphere of media activity today. Be it at the ideation, contemplation or creation stage, our private as well as public lives are suffused and saturated with the all pervading influence of social media. Which person, young, middle aged or even old, has not been informed of a post, a comment or confronted with a video uploaded on Facebook, or as it is known in its current avatar, Meta. Like it or not, you cannot escape the indomitable looming presence of social media and new media which is now, omni present. Consider this imaginary scene in a house. The wife is in the kitchen, cooking and talking to her friend on a WhatsApp video call, her husband is busy drinking tea and browsing through his Facebook friends page, the daughter is booking a Uber cab (which uses AI tools in their app). All knowingly or unknowingly, are using new media tools, to fulfil their desired ends. Most people equate new media with the only too obvious sectors such as IT, Telecom or the Entertainment Industry, but new media is now making its presence felt both anonymously and ubiquitous, everywhere. In the near future, by say, 2025, AI will step into every sector, be it retail marketing, cyber security or health care. It will also aid in making finance more inclusive and manufacturing more automated and less process and labour driven and more machine driven. Does that mean that there is going to be job displacement worldwide, leading to recession and unemployment in labour driven industries? Not necessarily. Darwin went to great pains to elaborately drive home the point that humans need to evolve and adapt in order to survive and in the age of the information revolution, this is only to be expected and accepted. Jobs will not disappear; it is just that the nature of jobs will change and manual repetitive tedious tasks will now give way to more creative, visionary and schedule driven tasks rather than labour intensive efforts. Of course, as Alvin Toffler has already reinforced his point in his books on the third and fourth wave, that every sea change in technology brings in its own challenges in its wake, the fifth wave where AI, machine learning and of course, machines would dominate, perhaps even transform the course of our lives as is obliquely indicated in so many science fiction books and movies in the past.

While most media channels lean heavily towards eulogising and glorifying the amazing benefits that will accrue as new media technologies and processes continue to be adopted in increasing measure, no media, be it new or old can exist without its "dark side". In fact a parallel world exists in cyberspace known as the "dark web' that many are not aware of.

And so it is that new media with its attendant benefits also brings with it, a new brood of cyber "vipers" or menaces. Even while writing this book, it would come as no surprise to me if after a few months of publication, an electronic (PDF) version of it would be available on pirated sites, all primed up and ready to be downloaded. Cyber piracy is a gargantuan behemoth that is costing the nation's exchequer, crores of rupees. Because piracy in all its malignant forms exists not only in the realms of books and magazines, it carries over to piracy of digital content, films, videos, websites and various forms of print media. Cyber piracy with its pros and cons is covered in chapter three in great length along with related subjects such as Intellectual Property rights which has now greatly debated issue with the inception of the digital domain. As mentioned earlier, while the world at large cannot stop applauding and praising the mesmerizing effect of a virtual reality immersive experience at a Las Vegas show or doctors in a hospital animatedly discuss with their colleagues at a medical convention the exciting new additional information available with new medical imaging and diagnostic techniques, we also have to deal with the ever present threat of cyber security which is now a matter of extreme concern with large multinationals, mega corps and giant business houses and banks, which have suffered massive revenue losses at the hands of a single individual who armed with just a few coding and programming skills can hack into giant servers and siphon off funds into his own personal account simply by running a few lines of complex code. Movies like "Hackers" "Firewall" and "War Games" have only too clearly highlighted the scope and nature of this problem, which has now become too humongous a threat to be ignored or set aside to be dealt with at a later stage.

All students of Journalism and Mass Communication would have at some stage of their studies have been introduced to the concept of "convergence" which is the present century propitious promise of all media converging onto a single compact platform which is none other than - yes you guessed right, the mobile instrument. Gone are the days of large super water cooled super computers and bulky desktop computers with a tangled mass of cables and wires writhing out of the various ports like a fancy hairdo gone amok. Today's computers are condensed into as small a gadget as a "smart" i watch or the latest gen iPhone. Gradually even laptops, compact and powerful though they may undoubtedly be, are giving way to their faster, cheaper and lighter (the motto of all the tech promoting giants) cousin, the "Smartphone". The new phones sport so many features already built in, and if some are missing, they can always be added at a later stage with an ever increasing horde of mobile apps, that there is no need to access bigger and heavier digital systems. Enter the super busy corporate executive who is dashing off message after message from an "outlook" app on his smart phone, or the acutely aware citizen journalist who is streaming "breaking news" at breakneck speeds from his mobile device, a topic explored in chapter eight which celebrates the dawn of a new age mediated conscience - the 'citizen journalist'.

In this book, we have just touched on the mind-bending possibilities and expanding reach of new media. As technology continues to grow, accelerate and reinvent itself, new media, with every new iteration will become more powerful, more relevant.

It is our sincere hope that this book will do just that - bridge the gap which exists between the hype and the fact, between the assumed and the actual, and demystify some hard to grasp concepts that assail the reader or viewer every time s/he picks up a newspaper or scours the Internet. We hope that reading this book will bring you as much pleasure as we experienced in exploring this exciting "new media" field, which as you would realize, is the pressing need of the hour

LIST OF FIGURES

Fig 1.1: Variety of social and other forms of new media 3

Fig 1.2. Branches of new media 6

Fig 3.1 Global revenue losses through piracy 30

Fig 3.2: Overview of International Treaties on Intellectual Property 33

Fig 4.1. Growth of social networking, yearly 43

Fig 4.2 Summary of social media popularity findings 50

Fig 5.1. Teenage Experience of Cyberbullying 65

Fig 5.2. Cyberbullying Experiences Differentiated by Gender 68

Fig 5.3. Impact of Cyberbullying 70

Fig 6.1: Importance of Technical Skills by 2020 86

Fig 6.2: Importance of Technical Skills by 2020 91

Figure 7.1 Taxonomy of Data Journalism 104

Figure 7.2 The stages of Data Journalism 107

Fig. 8.1 Number of Mobile Users in the World from 2020 to 2025 120

Fig. 8.2 Changing Media Consumption 128

Fig 9.1: Possible Applications of Artificial Intelligence 148

Fig 10.1: Global Augmented Reality and Virtual Reality Market 2021-2025 171

LIST OF TABLES

Table 5.1. Where Bullying Takes Place 61

Table 5.2. Experience of Cyberbullying 63

Table 7.1: Types of Data Journalism projects/
stories proposed by others 102

Table 9.1: Uses of Machine Learning 156

TABLE OF CONTENTS

1. Transitioning from Traditional Media to the Digital Realm 1
   Conclusion 7

2. Globalisation, Neo-Liberalism And The Public Sphere 9
   2.1 Theories on Globalisation and Neoliberalism 17
   2.2 Impact of Globalisation 19
   Conclusion 20
   References 20

3. Intellectual Property Rights, Copyrights and Cyber Piracy in the Digital Domain 21
   3.1 Traditional Intellectual Property Rights ... 21
   3.2 Copyright Protection Acts 24
   3.3 Copyright theft and Piracy 29
   3.4 Copyright Protection Act of India 33
   Conclusion 37
   References 39

4. Increasing Role of Social Media: Changes in Formats, Approaches and Transparency 40
   4.1 Introduction 40
   4.2 Meteoric rise of Data Survelliance 42
   4.3 Precautions to Adopt 44

	4.4	Role of Government and Governmental bodies 52
		National Security Imperatives 53
	4.5	Privacy Concerns and Civil Liberties 54
	4.6	Future of Private and Public Spaces 54
5.	Security at the crossroads; Invasion of personal spaces, cyber frauds, cyber bullying and harassment 57	
	5.1	Introduction 57
	5.2	Cyber harassment and Cyber bullying 58
	5.3	The Nature of Cyberbullying 59
	5.4	Effects of Cyberbullying and Cyberharrasment 69
		Conclusion 73
		References 75
6.	Rise of Consumerism, Digital Marketing and Click bait Consumerism 78	
	6.1	Factors contributing to the rise in consumerism 78
	6.2	Elements of Digital Marketing 79
	6.3	Social Media Dominance on Mobile 84
	6.4	Influencer Marketing impact on Mobile Marketing 85
	6.5	Mobile E-Commerce and M-Commerce . 85
	6.6	New Challenges and Opportunities 86
	6.7	Future of the digital market 91
		Conclusion 94

References 95

7. It's all about Data! Data Journalism, Data Analytics and Data Mining 96
    7.1 Data Journalism 96
    7.2 Types of Data Journalism 102
    7.3 Google Analytics 111
    Conclusion... 114
    References 115

8. Digital explorations of Civic Consciousness: The Evolution of Mobile Journalism 117
    8.1 Introduction.. 117
    8.2 The Rise of Mobile Journalism............... 118
    8.3 Ethical Concerns 122
    8.4 Innovations in Mobile Journalism.......... 124
    8.5 Challenges of Misinformation on Social Media... 127
    8.6 Mobile Journalism Internationally 129
    Conclusion... 133
    References 134

9. Artificial Intelligence and Machine Learning: The New Normal.. 136
    9.1 Introduction.. 136
    9.2 Foundations of AI and ML..................... 136
    9.3 Early Origins of Artificial Intelligence ... 140
    9.4 The importance of Big Data 144
    9.5 Applications of AI 148

    9.6   Machine Learning 152

    Conclusion 157

    References 158

10. Burgeoning of the Metaverse: VR and AR parallel worlds 159

    10.1 Introduction 159

    10.2 History of the Metaverse 161

    10. 3 Characteristics of the Metaverse 164

    10.4 Gaming and the Metaverse 170

    10.5 Non-Fungible Tokens (NFTs) 173

    Conclusion 175

    References 176

CHAPTER ONE

Transitioning from Traditional Media to the Digital Realm

Digital Media are communication technologies that enable or enhance interaction between users as well as interface between users and content. Traditional media tools like newspapers, radio and television that came before digital technology has always been there as a means of information, education and communication. Furthermore, it has also existed as a primary source of entertainment and relaxation.

The term 'New Media' is often a bone of contention and conflict, as new definitions and scope of the subject are constantly redefined and reinvented.

Among the key concerns was that the phrase is already dated, that there is actually very little 'new' about the so-called 'New Media' today. All media and technology have been at one time new, and so the implicit meaning of 'New Media' is transient at best. The next question that naturally followed was that if 'New Media' is actually old, then what should it be called? Although we may understand what we mean by 'New Media' today, its roots are clearly adopted from old media and most of the so-called changes in

New Media are basically integrating the new technologies and workflows that have now become part and parcel of the media pipeline and systems. Since New Media has been introduced some time back and is in danger of becoming old, throughout the course of this book, we will be using the term "digital media" is it is much more current and relevant although the words "New Media" and "Digital Media" have been often used interchangeably.

In the ever-evolving landscape of media consumption, the transition from old media to new media has become not just a trend but a necessity for survival. As technology continues to advance at a rapid pace, traditional forms of media such as print newspapers, radio, and television are facing unprecedented challenges. Meanwhile, new media platforms like social media, streaming services, and online publications are gaining momentum, reshaping the way information is disseminated and consumed. This shift presents both challenges and opportunities for media organizations and content creators alike.

Fig 1.1: Variety of social and other forms of new media
Source: https://carleton.ca/communityfirst/2017/5-tips-sharing-research-social-media/

Old media, characterized by its one-way communication model, has long been the primary source of information and entertainment for the masses. However, with the rise of new media, which emphasizes interactivity, customization, and user generated content, traditional media outlets are being forced to adapt or risk becoming obsolete. This transition entails not only technological upgrades but also a fundamental shift in mindset and strategy.

One of the key challenges in transitioning from old media to new media is the need to embrace digital technologies. Traditional media companies must invest in digital infrastructure, develop user-friendly platforms, and adopt innovative content delivery methods to stay relevant in today's digital age. This may involve restructuring internal processes, hiring digital-savvy talent, and forging strategic partnerships with tech companies.

Moreover, transitioning to new media requires a revaluation of content creation and distribution strategies. In the past, content was typically produced by professionals and disseminated through mass media channels. However, in the era of new media, anyone with an internet connection can create and share content with the world. This democratization of content creation presents both challenges and opportunities for media organizations.

On one hand, traditional media outlets must compete with a vast array of online content creators for audience attention. This requires them to produce high-quality, engaging content that resonates with their target audience. On the other hand, new media platforms offer unparalleled opportunities for content discovery and audience engagement. By leveraging social media, search engine optimization, and other digital marketing techniques, media organizations can reach a wider audience and build a loyal following online.

Another important aspect of transitioning to new media is the shift towards audience-centricity. Unlike old media, which often operated on a broadcast model with limited audience interaction, new media platforms thrive on user engagement and feedback. Media organizations must listen to their audience, understand their preferences and behaviours, and tailor their content and marketing efforts accordingly. This requires a more agile and data-driven approach to content creation and distribution. Whereas the old media was driven more by thoughts, opinions and authentic research to some extent (although this was not really a driving force), present media is not only heavily data and statistic driven, but also seems to more focus on fact checking and authenticity of information, rather than present an unbiased opinion or picture of the true scenario revolving around a story.

Furthermore, the monetization model for new media differs significantly from that of old media. While traditional media outlets relied primarily on advertising revenue and subscription fees, new media platforms offer a diverse range of revenue streams, including sponsored content, affiliate marketing, crowdfunding, and subscription-based services. Media organizations must explore new revenue opportunities and adapt their business models to thrive in the digital landscape.

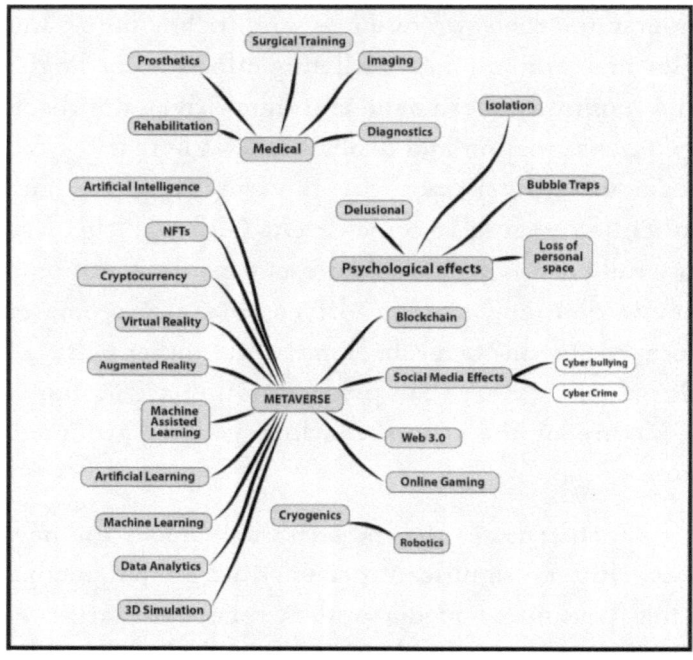

Fig 1.2. Branches of new media

Despite the challenges involved, transitioning from old media to new media also presents numerous opportunities for growth and innovation. By embracing digital technologies, media organizations can reach a global audience, experiment with new formats and storytelling techniques, and forge deeper connections with their audience. The rise of social media influencers, online streaming platforms, and digital-first media companies demonstrates the immense potential of new media to disrupt traditional media paradigms.

Moreover, new media offers greater flexibility and agility, allowing media organizations to adapt to changing market dynamics more quickly. With the ability to gather real-time data and analytics, content creators can measure audience engagement, track performance metrics, and iterate on their content strategy in real-time. This iterative approach to content creation enables media organizations to stay ahead of the curve and remain competitive in a fast-paced digital landscape.

Conclusion

In conclusion, the transition from old media to new media is not just a technological shift but a cultural and strategic transformation. Media organizations must embrace digital technologies, rethink their content creation and distribution strategies, and adopt a more audience-centric approach to thrive in today's digital age.

While speed of course is of the essence, the media industry need to understand and realize that the audience today is neither naïve nor uninformed. But the presence of fake news, deep fakes and channels such as Tik Tok have made the viewers and readers today extremely sceptical and critical of any news which even remotely smacks of sensationalism. It is absolutely imperative that media today recapture the element of trust and faith in the media, which today is sadly lacking. Technology and methods of presentation may have changed and real anchors replaced by artificial and synthetic AI anchors, but the audience even today is hungry not for fake or "synthetic" news, but real original and well narrated and knit original news stories. Once this becomes the norm of reporters, bureau chiefs and news networks, journalism and new media will once again recover the magic of news and news dissemination which dominated the seventies and eighties.

While the transition to new media today may present challenges, it also offers unprecedented opportunities for growth, innovation, and creativity. By embracing the digital era, media organizations can future-proof their businesses and continue to engage and inspire audiences in new and exciting ways.

CHAPTER TWO

GLOBALISATION, NEO-LIBERALISM AND THE PUBLIC SPHERE

Globalization and neo-liberalism are two interconnected forces that have profoundly shaped the contemporary world, influencing economic, political, and cultural landscapes. Globalization refers to the increasing interconnectedness and interdependence of countries through the exchange of goods, services, information, and ideas on a global scale. Neo-liberalism, on the other hand, is an economic and political ideology that advocates for free-market capitalism, limited government intervention, and the promotion of individual liberties. Over the past few decades, these forces have become central players in the ongoing narrative of the globalized world, sparking both enthusiasm and criticism.

With the advancement of technology, the abatement of full-fledged wars of the mid twentieth century, breakdown of trade and communication barriers, the phenomena of globalisation as well as of Liberalism and especially Neo-liberalism (the Greek word "Neo" means new) has received a lot of media as well as international governmental attention.

Although the two are often used together, there is a vast difference between the two. Globalisation is more of a phenomena or a movement, whereas Neo-liberalism is more of an ideology or a reciprocated response to the economic challenges which ensconced the mid twentieth century and finds its ideological roots in the thoughts and writings of great economists like Friedrich Hayek and Milton Friedman. They were both instrumental in bringing about a wealth of economic reform and questioned time honoured notions of free market economy and the so called "enslavement" that capitalism apparently brought in its wake.

Going by traditional definitions as is enshrined in the Oxford dictionary, globalisation can be stated as,

> "the process by which business start or operate on a global scale".

This is a very simplistic and narrow definition of globalization as now it encompasses a much more wider sphere of activity and hence the definition provided by Kozul-Wright and Rowthorn is more closer to the truth. These authors envision globalisation as

> ... an increase in the volume of cross-border economic interactions and resource flows, producing a qualitative shift in the relations between national economies and between nation-states (Baker et. al., 1998, p. 5; Kozul-Wright and Rowthorn, 1998, p.

1).

Others have defined it as,

> "the compression of the world and the intensification of consciousness of the world as a whole. (Robertson, 1992: 8)

The word "globalisation" itself gained agency and widespread usage after the launch of the path breaking media pioneer, Marshal McLuhan's book on the "The Medium is the Message" where, because of the apparent shrinking of distances as a result of a dramatic reduction in the time taken to traverse them, the entire world was conceived as one global village. In a typical visionary and futuristic style, Luhan envisaged the oncoming of the second great media phenomena of convergence where all technologies appear to be converging onto one single platform and that was - the digital one.

The phenomena is not a new one and all students of economics of trade and trade routes as well as students of political science will be aware that during the colonial era there was a great volume of trade between nations that was occurring and along with migration of people, opening up of new trade routes, also a great amount of exploitation of resources as well as human capital. It was these colonial processes that inspired great political thinkers like Karl Marx to emerge with the concept of the "Bourgeoise" and the

"Proletariat" and the exploitation of the weaker by the supposedly stronger work force.

Globalisation has given a major impetus to three kinds of economic interactions viz., merchandise trade flows, foreign direct investment, and cross-border financial investments. Even nonstudents of commerce and economics will be able to perceive fairly clearly that nations comprising of the world economy's industrial and capital rich core can greatly benefit the capital poor nations by lending at low interest rates, thereby greatly facilitating commerce and the exchange of goods and services. Of course, a valid argument repeatedly presented is that producers of domestic goods stand to lose, as they can in no way compete with either the price efficiency or the quality of goods imported, but again a counter argument can be advanced that this is exactly the impetus or push that is needed for internal goods producers to catch up or compete with the international market. Through enhancing both the quality and price offered so as to be on par with their international counterparts. But this seesaw argument belongs to the domain of international trade and is hardly relevant here except to provide a theoretical framework for the subject of media globalisation which we shall examine closely now.

Owing the interconnectedness and the rich cultural exchange that has been introduced through dramatic improvements in technology, especially internet technology, content creation has become easier than ever and not only can countries share content at the click of a mouse, so to speak, that content can also be monitored, filtered and edited with equal facile ease. Anyone with a novel and innovative idea can now become global entrepreneur and neither time nor age are anymore any real barriers. According to Manuel Castell (2010),

> " communication technology has a major role in the rise of networked society. Specialised doctors of other countries are now easily accessible, people can easily keep a check on the stock market, and online education has emerged as a boon for many students".

In 1977, a famous report familiar to all media students, known as the "MacBride Commission Report" was presented wherein the commission acknowledged the fact that there were huge "imbalances" in the flow of communication and recommended developed nations to encourage the democratization of communication, promote adult literacy and encourage all to exchange technical information so that technology or knowledge remains within the purview of a few elected but is in the common domain of all. A neo-liberal approach to globalization is a little different from general theories of globalization. Andrei Volodin believes that globalization will fulfil all humanistic requirements only in a, "truly pluralistic democratic society where power is accountable and decentralized".[1]

Many examples of the good as well as the bad effects of globalization can be cited here. A case in point which comes to immediate recollection is the coverage provided by the "Irish Times" of the Sudanese crisis in the war zone of Bahr-el-Ghazal. There were very different ideological perspectives present in the reporting of this crisis that took place between the Muslim dominated north and the Christian and animist south. At the heart of all the criticisms and reporting of globalization either in the North or Southern regions are viewpoints centering on how capitalism lies at the very epicentre of Globalisation and is often one of the "prime movers" in any transnational movements that give rise to globalization. Consumerism is heavily promoted by media industries as well as identifying or 'labelling' what is regarded as a desirable lifestyle and body type and body image. Ownership patterns further complicate the issue and hence we find transnational companies controlling diverse goods and services that are offered in the free market. TNCs play a major role in manufacturing and extractive activities and are important actors in increased flows of capital across nation states which is perhaps one of the most significant features of globalization.

Another aspect of globalization is the cultural homogenization that takes place, on a universal scale.

The new Indie pop culture seamlessness pervades all strata of urban youth and the new digital audio MP3 genre of music has ubiquitously captured the global pop market.

Burnett (1996) undertook a detailed analysis of the global record industry of six dominant companies viz. Time Warner, Sony, Phillips, Matsushita and Thorn-EMI.

Based on the findings of his study, Burnett concluded that

> "globalization is not a homogenous process and that "extreme privatization and economic competition would, in the long run, lead to instability".[2]

Gobalisation also changed the way that media systems and structures traditionally operated. According to Bagdikian and

Curran (2023) key trends that emerged were,

> "…emergence of global conglomerations; Horizontal and Vertical integration and diversification, synergy and technological convergence".[3]

Ownership can be vertical or horizontal. In the case of horizontal ownership, often the parent company may have little or no logical relationship with the company that it owns. For example, Reliance which is into multiple business and corporate establishments also owns CNN-IBN, a media house. This has greatly contributed to the commercialization of the media, and as the big business houses are financially controlling the media houses, the latter have literally no say in many matters and the corporate intervention may even extent to the kind of media coverage put out by the print or electronic media house.

Vertical ownership on the other hand, sometimes also known as chain ownership, is when the exact opposite occurs, and there is some relationship of the child company to the parent company.

In recent years, globalisation theories by itself are not regarded as sufficient to explain many economic and political movements across nations. This has given rise to a many neo-liberal ideologies which encompass both economic as well as normative ideals of society. Interest in this topic has arisen as it influences global mental health also in many ways. Many theories have arisen regarding globalisation and its relation with mental health, amongst one of which is the argument propounded by Kirmayer and Minas (2000) who averred that it did have an impact on collective as well as individual identity and shaped the "dissemination of psychiatric knowledge" worldwide.

Other studies have emerged with bolder, more definitive associations like the one conducted by Pickett, James and Wilkinson who in 2006, showed fairly conclusively by collecting data from eight welfare economy countries that there was,

"... a strong linear association between income inequality and the prevalence of mental illness" and also clearly indicated that there was a strong effect size for serious mental illness. Another study posited the fairly surprising argument that "schizophrenia rates are higher in countries with greater inequality[4] (Burns, Tomita, and Kapadia 2014) (Glob&Neo Structural Determinants, P. 5: 2034).

2.1 Theories on Globalisation and Neoliberalism

Globalisation theories have assumed even greater importance because of the increasing role of convergence. Old and new media technologies are now converging on digital platforms, raising new challenges for media practitioners as well as students. It also enables human beings to become more aware, more sensitive to their environments and reflect on their own environment vis-a-vis other social and political climates. But despite all the obvious claims and boasts of globalization, it has more than its fair share of critics. Some like John Pilger label the protagonists of globalisation as the "new rulers of the world" who are exploiting both raw materials as well as labour power of the "poorest of the poor". Others are vociferous in pointing out that globalisation is completely bound up with ties of consumerism and hence contributes to the ebb and flow of capitalism and related ideologies.

Another commonly debated concept is whether the benefits of globalization and neo-liberalism are equitably distributed. Most believe that it (globalisation) has contributed to alleviating poverty and equitable distribution of income, while the majority of public opinion is of the view that globalisation has only increased the GDP of already wealthy nations and has only contributed to filling the coffers of wealthy scions while the vast majority has only become more impoverished and dependent on their capitalist masters. Most believe that increased flow of goods and services and an overarching profit motive only comes at the expense of depletion of resources as the capitalists and wealth mongers of the world reroute these resources into their own private domains. And also, an offshoot consequence is increasing environmental degradation as natural resources are destroyed to make place for artificial ones

On a cultural level, the fear of cultural homogenization and the loss of diversity is a recurring criticism of globalization. As Western cultural products dominate the global market, there is a concern that indigenous cultures and languages may be marginalized or lost. This has sparked movements advocating for cultural preservation and the recognition of diverse voices in the global cultural landscape.

2.2 Impact of Globalisation

The impacts of globalization and neo-liberalism are multifaceted and extend across various aspects of society. Economically, globalization has led to increased economic growth and the lifting of millions of people out of poverty in developing countries. However, it has also contributed to income inequality both within and between nations. The outsourcing of jobs to low wage countries and the concentration of wealth in the hands of a few global corporations are notable examples of this trend.

Neo-liberal economic policies have likewise generated mixed results. Proponents argue that these policies have stimulated economic growth, increased efficiency, and created opportunities for innovation. However, critics point to the widening wealth gap, job insecurity, and the erosion of workers' rights as negative consequences of neo-liberalism. The 2008 global financial crisis, often attributed to lax financial regulations and excessive risktaking, highlighted the vulnerabilities inherent in the neo-liberal economic model.

On a political level, globalization has led to the formation of international institutions and agreements designed to regulate global interactions. While these mechanisms aim to promote cooperation and prevent conflict, they have also faced criticism for favouring the interests of powerful nations and corporations.

Neoliberalism's influence on political systems is evident in the push for limited government intervention, with privatization and deregulation often leading to reduced social services and the concentration of economic power.

Conclusion

Culturally, both globalization and neo-liberalism have had profound effects. The spread of information and ideas on a global scale has led to cultural homogenization in some aspects, with Western values and consumer culture becoming pervasive. However, this has also sparked cultural hybridization and resistance, as communities strive to preserve their unique identities in the face of global influences. Neo-liberalism's emphasis on individual liberties has contributed to the commodification of culture, as cultural products become market driven commodities rather than expressions of identity and creativity.

References

Chhibber, B. (2007). Globalisation and International relations: Changing paradigms.

Watson, A. (2008). Global music city: knowledge and geographical proximity in London's recorded music industry. Area, 40(1), 12-23.

McManus, J. H. (2009). The commercialization of news. The handbook of journalism studies, 218-233.

CHAPTER THREE

Intellectual Property Rights, Copyrights and Cyber Piracy in the Digital Domain

3.1 Traditional Intellectual Property Rights

Intellectual Property as media concept, let alone legally enshrined concept and statute was unknown prior to the "Digital Divide". Before the advent of photocopiers, publishing and printing of books was extremely limited and to copy a book, meant you had to go back to the printers and request a new copy. With the invention and introduction of photocopying machines (its introduction began in the early fifties), duplication of copyrighted material become not only easier, it even became fashionable, especially amongst college students because of the tremendous cost reduction and the fact that hard to access books, papers and other documents pertaining to their field of study could now be easily accessed, reproduced and stored. And thus arose the early beginnings of piracy and the tangled tale of copyrights and intellectual property and scaffolded within it, the ethical and moral dimensions to this intricate issue.

Before delving deeper into the convoluted issues of intellectual property, it is important to have a "textbook" definition of it. Since Intellectual Property is no longer confined to mere semantics, and now encompasses legal ramifications, there needs to be a clear definition of its scope.

Laws vary on this subject from continent to continent and US laws on Intellectual property are somewhat different from that enshrined in our own constitution.

In U.S. law, the idea of intellectual property was drafted directly into the Constitution. Outlining the powers of Congress, Article I, Section 8 states simply, "To promote the Progress of Science and useful Arts, by securing for limited Times to Authors and Inventors the exclusive Right to their respective Writings and Discoveries. The protection of intellectual property was used as a means to incentivise the production of new ideas.

Intellectual Property Rights actually began to receive serious attention after the Berne Convention which was established in 1886 in Berne, Switzerland. 105 countries are members of this convention with India also being one of the members of Berne Convention. To prevent copyright infringements, it is strongly suggested that copyrights should be registered. Registration is made, in person or via a representative, with the Copyright Office. Since 2016, copyright policy was moved to India's Ministry of Commerce and Industry. Currently, all IPRs are now administered by the Department for Industrial

Property and Promotion (DIPP).[1] Intellectual Property Rights received a firm grounding through the WTO agreement on Trade Related Aspects of Intellectual Property Rights more popularly known as TRIPS.

> "In the Uruguay Round of talks, multilaterally, governments established an agreed framework for recognizing and enforcing IPRs both in the national and international contexts".

Industries in collaboration with governments have partnered with institutions such as the World Intellectual Property

Organisation (WIPO), the World Customs Organisation (WCO) and also Interpol, in order to enhance enforcement.

Along with the Copyright Protection Act, another Act to grant security and a certain measure of protection to the IT industry is the Information Technology Act of 2000 which was primarily framed to prevent piracy. In the last five years, they have been instrumental in shutting down 630 illegal Internet sites. But, by and large, they are not effective. In fact, to make the laws relevant, the government recently amended the Acts to make the laws stricter and bring more online crimes under its purview.

One of the primary reasons why Intellectual Property has emerged as such as an essential safeguard in modern times is on account of the threat of increasing piracy, both in India as well as internationally. Several organisations have emerged to deal with the threat of intellectual property theft, the foremost being the World Intellectual Property Organisation (WIPO) who have developed several treaties to help assist in the protection of copyright. This organisation defines piracy as being "associated with infringements of copyright or related rights'; and the term is 'normally used in connection with cases of intentional infringements of IP rights, related to commercial purposes of the infringer, or causing significant economic harm to the right holder (Crisp, 2013)."

3.2 Copyright Protection Acts

Copyright violations and theft of Intellectual Property have now become so common and rampant that there was felt a pressing need was to set up an organisation that would counter these threats and address it on a war footing and so an organisation was set up known as TRIPS, The Agreement on Trade-Related Aspects of Intellectual Property Rights which began at the end of the Uruguay Round of the General Agreement on Tariffs and Trade (GATT) between 1989 and 1990. This is an international legal agreement between all the member nations of the World Trade Organization (WTO). TRIPS establish certain minimum standards for protection and provides guidelines for enforcement of these standards. Under their umbrella, computer programs are also protected under copyright laws as literary works.

At various points of time, other acts have been introduced such as the Protect IP Act, but all these have only been of limited value as deterrent mechanisms that can only deflect or delay piracy but cannot really stop it. Nathan Fisk has correctly stated that:

> "Ultimately, the world of intellectual property is far from clear-cut. It is messy and always shifting. Overall, what is important is striking a balance between the rights of authors and the rights of consumers. The ongoing tension between the two is what allows the system of intellectual property laws to work, and giving over too much power to either the author or the consumer may result in severely limited production of creative works for everyone".[2]

Why are copyrights and IPR gaining so much prominence in the current scenario? Perhaps the answer lies in the shift from physical replication to copying and replication in the digital world. What was earlier a cumbersome process has now been reduced to a few mouse clicks.

Copyright laws serve as potential "gatekeepers", filtering what content users can access on the Internet. In the US, section 107 of the Copyright Act includes four factors that govern what is termed as "fair use". These include the nature of the copyrighted work, what percentage of the copyrighted material will be reproduced in proportion to the complete original work and the effect the use of the work will have on the potential market for the copyrighted work.

There are two factors that need to be considered when it comes to consumption of information. Firstly, it is essentially non-rival which means that usage of intellectual property by one person does not decrease the possibility of use by others.

Secondly, information or intellectual property goods may be non-excludable in the sense that the producer of intellectual property goods is often unable to exclude non-payers from consuming goods without due authorization.[3]

In India, the Copyright Act was introduced in 1957, with subsequent amendments to the Act in 1994 and 1995. This was essential since as usage and consumption of digital media proliferated, and digital piracy began to spread its ubiquitous tentacles, amendments pertaining to limitations and sanctions had to be continually added and updated.

Both private and government investments and expenditure on software are extremely high and so is the extent of piracy, and hence is a matter of increasing concern. Business Software Alliance, a US based research organization, brings out reports every year that tabulates the different areas in which piracy is occurring and the losses accruing to the government exchequer as a consequence.

The Copyright (Amendment) Act of 1994 explicitly specifies the extent of fines or punishment when the Copyright Act is infringed or violated. Furthermore, the Law prohibits unauthorised duplication of software, or giving copies of that software or other digital goods to another individual which has not been legally purchased. Within a particular organisation the consumer is not permitted to distribute non-authorised copies of digital content. The laws of the Working Draft of December 2, 1996 of University of California Copyright Legislation and Scholarly Communication spells out restrictions on copyright and intellectual property quite stringently

> "Copyright law provisions for digital works should maintain a balance between the interests of creators and copyright owners and the public that is equivalent to that embodied in current statute. The existing legal balance is consonant with the educational ethic of responsible use of intellectual properties, promotes the free exchange of ideas, and protects the economic interests of copyright holders". [4]

Piracy is not a new phenomenon and has a long and chequered history. And although it has now moved away from debauchery and renegade pirates on the high seas to the computer and supercomputer, this has in no way, mitigated the seriousness of the crime. Initially this term was only loosely applied to highway robbers and criminals who ruled the waves, but after the invention of the printing press, this term became applicable to all those who made unapproved or unauthorised copies of any manuscript that was published.

The state recognises this and hence has introduced many laws to curtail at least the extent, if not intensity, of this crime, but there are many caveats in its implementation.

Digital piracy is a growing menace and although so many agencies and laws have been introduced to curb this societal hazard. Digital Rights Management or DRM works by a system of watermarking and online product registration and so-called "decoy" strategies which attempt to restrict usage and sharing of files, but at best these restraints serve only as delays and obstacles (much like the "nag screens" we see on websites) that make it difficult, but in no way, render it impossible to pirate or replicate digital material. However Digital Rights Management has created more confusion than copyright protection. The whole process of implementing and managing digital rights is very cumbersome and the tedious process of authentication, managing all the region settings and also restrictions on the number of installations deter potential consumers from purchasing legal content, and they very often prefer pirated products where all the consumer has to do is to download material using a VPN or other protocol scrambling device and then simply install the software or download content onto one's computer. In western countries, DRM has for the most part, has scored more failure rates than success and in India and Asian countries it is almost unheard of.

The alternative to accessing and downloading illegal material is piracy and although Telecom Regulatory Authority of India (TRAI) has redoubled its efforts to crack down on piracy, it still is a major problem. It is generally perceived that piracy is creating chaos in the content industry since there are no curbs or authorisation needed when one is surfing or downloading content through peer-to-peer networks and through the huge underground world of the "Darknet". Professor Richard Epstein attributes reasons for this failure because,

"virtually all of the current malaise in dealing with both tangible and intellectual property stems from the failure to keep to the coherent rules of acquisition, exclusion, alienation, regulation, and condemnation that are called for by the classical liberal system ..." (Menell, P.S., 2010).[5]

3.3 Copyright theft and Piracy

Copyright theft and piracy is a massive problem not just in Asian countries but in the US as well. It is estimated that In1996, US copyright based industries lost approximately $10.7 billion to pirates outside of the US.

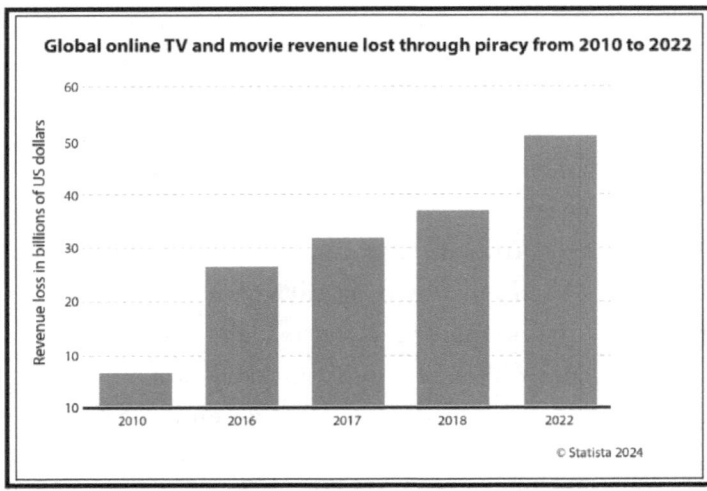

Fig 3.1 Global revenue losses through piracy
Source: Statista.com

Some sociologists explain piracy in India as intrinsically acceptable since our entire social system and ancestry in deeply embedded in the joint family system and hence sharing comes as a naturally corollary to our very existence and work culture. But this is simply at attempt to rationalise a reprehensible act, and no court of law or IT or IT related organisation will justify this logic through any stretch of the imagination.

In India this is not so common, but in the US, there has been a continuing and concerted effort to curtail piracy, and this often manifests itself in the form of takedowns of pirated websites from time to time. A famous case in the US is of Viacom company taking down a video posted by Christopher Knight on

Youtube which was apparently an flagrant infringement of copyright laws, thus alleged the well-known company Viacom Inc. They issued a DMCA takedown request, and accordingly in the month of August in 2007, Knight received a mail from Youtube that his video of the VH1 segment had been removed. The way DMCA operates that is whenever a takedown notice is sent to the perpetrator of the copyright violation, another counter notice must be sent by the copyright owner. Only then can the takedown occur. Many other takedowns have occurred at various points of time, with varying degrees of success. Another infamous and extensive story doing the rounds involved the famous "Paranormalist", Uri Geller. Geller supposedly was endowed with such supernatural powers that he could bend spoons, forks and other metallic objects simply through the power of his mind. When a video tube video was posted showing how easily Geller's tricks could easily be replicated, Geller, in spite of consulting many, could not counter the worldwide criticism this video produced, so in order to salvage his declining reputation, he proceeded to do the next best thing, to recover lost respect, and that was to initiate a DMCA takedown. Eventually, the Electronic Frontier foundation also was forced to collaborate in a law suit against Geller, and after many deliberations the video was removed.

Although DMCA takedowns have enjoyed a degree of success, this has proved to large extent ineffectual and in oriental countries, it is virtually unknown. In India, the Telecom Regulatory Act of India (TRAI) has been much more successful in curbing piracy, and this along with SOPA (Stop Online Piracy Act) has slowed down, online piracy in its tracks.

The state of Kerala set up an Anti-piracy cell which works under the state Crime Branch Crime Investigation Department, and is fairly proactive in attempting to trace down systematic instances of piracy and copyright infringements. Other near stringent measures that have been adopted are orders such as the "John Doe Order" where the identity of the accused person is unknown at the time of filing a complaint and the accused can barely be identified as only a small description of the accused is documented. This order has been appropriated to a considerable extent by the Indian Film Industry which constantly faces the threat of online piracy and is completely devastated by torrent releases of their movies well before they are commercially released.

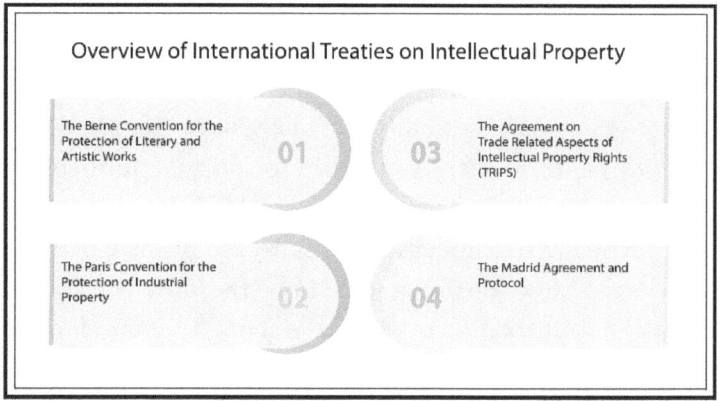

Fig 3.2: Overview of International Treaties on Intellectual Property
Source: FasterCapital.com
https://fastercapital.com/content/Intellectual-Property-Rights-in-the-Global-Arena--Understanding-International-Treaties.html

3.4 Copyright Protection Act of India

Copyright in India is less complex, but nevertheless there are definite laws that lay down unambiguous instructions on the creation and spread of intellectual property; the rights that govern it and how to protect them. A booklet on this tricky subject in India brought out by the Intellectual Property Rights office, reports the findings of a study performed to assess the progress of IPRs during 2006 - 2007 and 2018-2019. Experts selected from forty well known research organisations stated that research organisations do not have a formal and uniform process for commercialisation. Hence, appropriate estimation of economic values of existing technology and innovation are difficult in research organizations

A copyright is essentially a right where the author is "authorised" under the law to copy, publish or perform written or artistic works of Art. It provides the author with a specific license to use his or her work wherever they desire, since it is their own original creation, but forbids others from using that work in an creative endeavour unless they have sought special permission from the author to incorporate a part or the whole of the work. In physical works of art this is fairly easy to secure and to detect, but with the introduction of the digital domain, and the ease with which a work of art or writing can be reproduced has greatly complicated the issue

Copyright refers to two types of commodities – information or intellectual property goods – having certain characteristics.

Consumption of information related material have two very important features, Firstly, it is essentially non-rival in the sense that the use that one person makes of a piece of intellectual property does not decrease the possibility of use by others.

Second, information or intellectual property goods may be non-excludable in the sense that the producer of intellectual property goods is often unable to exclude non-payers from consuming goods without due authorization (Andrés - 2006 - The relationship between copyright software protec.pdf, n.d.).

Whenever copyright infringement is referred to, we need to understand what is meant by this. This literally means,

> "… in relation to a literary, dramatic, musical or artistic work, a reproduction thereof otherwise than in the form of a cinematographic film; (ii) in relation to a cinematographic film, a copy of the film made on any medium by any means;
>
> (iii) in relation to a sound recording, any other recording embodying the same sound recording, made by any means".

Although most regard copyright only in the context of print, the Copyright Act is very comprehensive and covers not just print, but audio such as original musical compositions and scores, original videos of any format and also live events, such as concert which may be photographed or filmed.

Copyright laws and Intellectual Property Rights received considerable media attention after the "Napster" fiasco when after the introduction of mp3 technology, thanks to the pioneering efforts of Sean Parker, an American entrepreneur and philanthropist, the software "Napster" developed by him was instrumental in shifting online piracy from a subversive underground activity to a commonly followed mainstream pursuit.

The copyright act also covers copyright of all original films made in India in any dialect or language. Apart from protecting the entertainment industry, the Act also protects the software industry and any kind of unauthorised copying or reproduction of commercial or customised software is highly condemned by the law and subject to jurisdiction and penalties. In India, according to section 63B, there is now minimum jail term of 7 days which can extend upto 3 years depending upon the scale and extent of piracy and fines range all the way from Rs. 50,000/- and depending on the discretion of the courts can also be scaled upward to as high a figure as two lakh rupees. This may not be completely successful in putting a halt to blatant piracy, but certainly serves as a deterrent. When one regards deterrents to piracy, there are many theories as to how effective, or how not effective, these deterrents are in reality. Scholars such as Schaub and Hawkins have proposed a theory which posits that individuals are rational actors who deliberately make choices to engage in illegal behaviour. (Gunter, 2009; Higgins et al., 2005; Lee and Lee, 2002).

The theory goes on to state that such errant behaviour can be restrained by the fear of punishment (Yoo et al., 2014). This is of course true of any illegal or criminal activity, not just software piracy. This truism is further reinforced by other researchers who aver that obtaining or purchasing pirated software is an illegal activity that is punishable by law (Morton and Koufteros, 2008). The way the legal mechanism works is to file a suit against the alleged infringer and then put in a claim for damages. The person receiving the legal notice could be an individual or owner of a website that encourages and facilitates illegal copying or torrenting downloads. Much has been written and much has been said about deterrents to piracy, but such nefarious activities to continue to persist, regardless. Various theories also have been propounded in the realm of psychology such as the "Theory of Planned Behaviour" (TPB) and the "Theory of Reasoned Action" (TRA) which does attempt to explain and interpret the mind of the perpetrator of the cybercrime but it of absolutely no help in curbing or halting the inexorable march of online piracy

> "... through an extended model of TPB that incorporates deterrence and expected utility theory, Peace et al. (2003) found that attitudes, PBC, and subjective norms were indeed significant in predicting the intention to illegally copy software".[6]

Conclusion

Intellectual Property Rights, Cyber piracy and Copyright Infringements are three sides of a prickly online dilemma for which no easily implementable solution exists at present. One of the reasons why this peculiar form of crime is so difficult to detect and curb is that, like hacking, it is undertaken by persons who are experts in Internet protocols, server hubs, domain control and other technical Knick knacks that exist in cyberspace, and most of the perpetrators of these crimes are often highly educated and intelligent cyber pirates. There are not only experts in navigating and mastering cyberspace but also are very well informed about the legal system that exists in their own country, the law of the land, so to speak and know, only too well, how to circumvent them. While theories about the need and the desire to pirate might provide a psychological framework that probes the mind of the infringer or pirate, they do little to restrain or restrict or even eliminate the problem. Legal actions like Copyright Laws, SOPA and other governmental agreements such as TRIPS (Trade Related Intellectual Property Rights) do make provisions to ensure protection of property rights for member countries, these are rarely adhered to nor is there the requisite commitment to transparency that is required for these agreements and enforcements to be really effective. So until there is a real awakening of civic conscience and a realization on the part of the consumer that they are depriving or rather, robbing the nation of an important source of revenue from IT related fields, this deplorable practice will continue. Central and State cyber cells and other bodies instituted to constrain cybercrime need to redouble their efforts if losses to the state exchequer are to be minimised.

References

[1] Intellectual property rights in India: Overview | practical law. (n.d.-a). https://uk.practicallaw.thomsonreuters.com/0-610-9089?contextData=(sc.

[2] Fisk, N. (2011). Digital Piracy. Infobase Publishing.

[3] Andrés, A. R. (2006). The relationship between copyright software protection and piracy: Evidence from Europe. European Journal of Law and Economics, 21, 29-51

[4] Basic Principles for Managing Intellectual Property in the Digital

Environment, Political Science and Politics, Sep., 1997, Vol. 30, No. 3 (Sep., 1997), pp. 570 – 574

[5] Menell, P. S. (2010). Governance of Intellectual Resources and Disintegration of Intellectual Property in the Digital Age. SSRN Electronic

Journal. https://doi.org/10.2139/ssrn.1615193

[6] Robertson, K., McNeill, L., Green, J., & Roberts, C. (2012). Illegal downloading, ethical concern, and illegal behaviour. Journal of business ethics, 108, 215-227

CHAPTER FOUR

Increasing Role of Social Media: Changes in Formats, Approaches and Transparency

4.1 Introduction

In the book "New Media and Society", author Deana A. Rohlinger makes a compelling observation. She says,

> "Have you ever felt like you are being watched by invisible eyes as you walk down the grocery aisle? In some ways, you are being watched. The grocery store is monitoring what you buy and how often you buy it. It's called dataveillance, which refers to the monitoring of our actions online and through our communication devices".[1]

Dataveillance or minute tracking of our online activities is rapidly becoming a rising scourge of new media activities in our current century. In the book the author mentions the ubiquity of on-line surveillance. Whether it be theme parks social or religious institutions, public forums or in the privacy of our home laptops or Desktops, mini bots, trackers and complex algorithms keep following or "tracking" every mouse click, every keystroke and browser button clicks as you navigate the world wide web. We live in an age of near complete transparency and privacy or the practice of attempting to conceal any net based activity is well nigh impossible. Initially, the motive of Big Data companies appeared to be purely commercial motives (keeping track of buying habits) so that gentle seemingly harmless suggestions can be made of what appropriate follow up could be made of online purchases or suggesting accessories that might possibly complement your immediate purchase.

But ceaseless monitoring of all your surfing has transgressed boundaries of commerce and political interest and has now invaded every sphere of activity of the careless netizen. Websites visited, purchases made, comments and posts transmitted, serious and casual WhatsApp chats, every comment, every image that is sent or viewed, comes under the public radar.

Every time photos or videos are uploaded on WhatsApp, Snapchat or Flickr, they are all tagged with personal information which is recorded and stored on huge databases (Big Data) for retrieval at a later date when the need arises.

This is the age of Big Data, and buying and selling of data, profiles and hitherto extremely confidential and sensitive information has now become commonplace and profitable. So long as your data remains within the confines of the server, there really is no problem, but the real problem arises when the data becomes public and identities are disclosed. In general, two types of identities disclosure exist. Identity disclosure and attribute disclosure, while somewhat different in nature and usage, constitutes a serious breach of privacy and personal protection.

Whenever information is made public, this information can in so many ways, be detrimentally used against the person who has wittingly or unwittingly made himself vulnerable to a variety of attacks. There have been cases, where a vacation plan has been made public on the social media and this plan has been used to advantage by thieves who break in during the period of absence of the owners.

To protect against these dangerous and incriminating disclosures, various protection techniques to anonymise user generated social media data have been devised, which will be examined in the next section.

4.2 Meteoric rise of Data Survelliance

Part of the reason of the increase in data mining and surveillance is because of the rapid proliferation and unprecedented growth of social media sites.

> "Skogerbo and Krumsvik argue that social media have become part of a networked and increasingly hybrid public sphere (2015), and that 'by their sheer ubiquity, these media contribute towards changing media ecologies and open new ways and forms of communication between citizens and their representatives" (p. 350)[2]

One of the most popular sites and very frequently accessed sites, Facebook, reached 1 million users in less than a year, fifty million in three and a half years and 500 million in six years, according to studies conducted by the Pew Research Centre.

Other social media sites like Twitter,

> "... reached 50 million in just two years. In 2018, Facebook claimed 2.23 billion monthly active users (Castillo, 2018)".[3]

Another research conducted in 2015 states that Facebook has more than 1.31 billion mobile users and 1.49 active users.[4]

The chart below shows the rapid growth of social media sites.

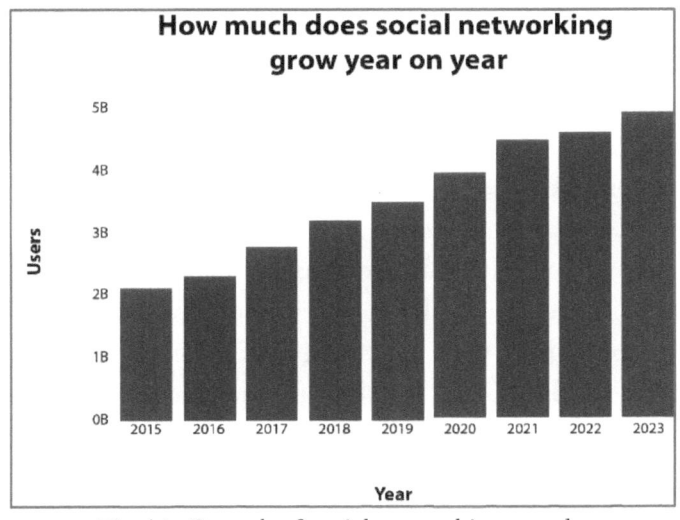

Fig 4.1. Growth of social networking, yearly
Source: backlinko.com https://backlinko.com/social-media-users

The reason why Facebook amongst the plethora of social media sites is still one of the most dangerous sites is because of its humungous database. In 2018, this site allowed Cambridge Analytica to access personal information on 87 million Facebook users. In doing so, Facebook had violated the 2011 Consent Order with the FTC, which stated that it was unlawful for any social media site to disclose user data without affirmative consent. This is only one of the instances of sites invoking breach of privacy norms. Regardless, it appears most of these violations that do occasionally happen, do not really affect the end user who continues to use and navigate social media sites with a fair amount of confidence.

4.3 Precautions to Adopt

Without a shadow of doubt, Surveillance and Dataveillance is nowhere on the decline. In fact, in the future, it will only increase. If you are wondering what are the essential differences between the two, Surveillance collects data from computer systems and the internet in general, whereas Dataveillance essentially gleans data from social media sites. If both of these are a given from which there is no escape for the consumer, then how can s/he best protect their interests, their business, their financial assets and their privacy? One of the most common and preferred methods currently is usage of a VPN. A VPN is instrumental in piping an intermediary server between the user and the site that is being connected to and browsed. Essentially the VPN scrambles internet protocols and conceals the identity of the net user. The monitoring agency can see that data is being accessed, even assess the quantum of data being accessed - uploaded or downloaded, but they cannot trace the user. Many VPNs are currently available in the market, making speed of internet traffic and level of encryption and security as their prime USP.

A simple common-sense approach is to approach social media sites with caution and well-grounded trepidation. This is needed since so many scams exist about how lives have been completely controlled and destroyed through excessive social media usage, a good case in point being the Indian film "Hacked" which exposed the extent of damage that hacking social media sites could create and implement.

> "Knowledge is a powerful tool, and if employees knew that social media postings may result in claims of defamation, discrimination, harassment, and invasion of privacy, they just might self- police the issue and make it a non-issue". [5]

Also, as one can very easily infer, common sense should prevail in any engagement with the media, social or otherwise. Some ground rules need to be established as to what should and can be posted and what is absolutely taboo. Author Melody Karle mentions five precautions that are absolutely mandatory to protect yourself and others from social media abuse. Some of the things never to post on Social Media Sites are:

- Photos of yourself at home, unless you know how to remove the embedded location in the photographs, or you know the platform removes it for you.

- Naked or sexual photos of yourself or anyone else. This is not only dangerous but also is against the user agreement rules for most social media accounts.

- Travel plans, especially if you live alone. This can invite break-ins while you are away.

- Home address and phone number. If people are your friends, they likely already know this information. If they don't, send them a direct message rather than posting this information to a large audience.

- Financial status or information, such as how much you make, photos of cash or valuables, or implications that you are a good target for theft or scams.

Many find the rules of engaging with social media content so complex and prohibitive that they avoid them altogether. Author Carla Mooney in her book, "Online Privacy and Social Media"[6] states that in one

Pew Research Center Report, twenty-seven percent of adults do not participate in social media platforms altogether. They of course, do use the internet (in the current context, life without the Internet is unthinkable), but avoid any kind of usage of any social media site. Those who do not take recourse to this rather extreme step, take other more practical, yet effective measures. They delete unwelcome or controversial posts the earliest, are very cautious about what comments or photos they post, many control the privacy settings of their social media app, and adjust privacy settings, status etc on the apps they use the most. All these precautionary measures can still be circumvented by someone with a little more than perfunctory knowledge of internet-based applications, but that is a risk all social media users need to take.

At a government or corporate level there are distinct software and protocols that can monitor social media sites, so that sensitive information is not leaked out or to at least ensure that such kind of breaches do not again occur in the future

> "After the 2013 bombing at the Boston Marathon, which killed 3 people and left 260 people wounded, local law enforcement used Dataminr to try to ensure that the event, which attracts thousands of people each year, was not attacked again".[7]

Dataminr is an AI based software tool that is highly useful in predicting high risk events so that catastrophic events can be either averted or the list of casualties minimised.

This tool can be used for any websites, including social media websites, as was done during the 2013 bombing at the Boston Marathon.

But to only indicate the negative side or aspects of SMSs (Social Media Sites) would be a biased and extremely one-sided view. Apart from the very obvious appeal of connectivity and having innumerable online friends, these sites are now playing a unique role in acting as surveillance instruments to augment police investigations and technology mediated policing. Since digital content is becoming harder to destroy or conceal (even hard disks where the data has been seemingly destroyed can be regurgitated and the data recovered through sophisticated customised software), investigations can be carried out successfully through the intervention of social media.

> "Access to digital content that is harder to destroy or conceal enhances investigations and, with the concomitant rise of crowdsourcing, big data, and computer analytics, facilitates networked, automated, and predictive surveillance".[8]

But is constant use of social media or even overuse, a necessarily bad side effect? There are many positive benefits and advantages of social media apart from the obvious ones like keeping in touch with friends or relatives, widening your portfolio or expanding your network. Social media far from widening the generation gap can diminish it. Through social media, especially apps like WhatsApp, parents can track what their children are doing, elder members of family can keep track of their peers or of their progeny. And all corporate executives and NGO employees are aware of the near constant stream of messages and communications that traverse the airwaves as employers and the employed, as peer groups, trainers and trainees constantly communicate with each other to facilitate schedules and production pipelines. For those with a sagging self-image or self concept, social media can bolster their confidence to a considerable extent without the need to go to a counsellor, psychiatrist or guru. Peer group acceptability is a *sine qua non* in today's excessive visual and digital culture, and this can be influenced to a great extent through posts and opinions garnered from the world wide web. Online gaming either through social media sites or by accessing internet gaming sites is a common platform for bond building and fostering new relationships. The Pew Research Foundation found that

> " boys often share their gaming handle with others with whom they would like to develop friendships and that seventy-one percent of boys use voice connections so that they can collaborate, chat, and trash talk with others while they play. These connections seem to be good for ontological security".

Not only new relationships built, explored and possibly maintained through the net but even the creation and sustaining of a virtual identity are catalysed through social media channels Say the authors of "New Media - A Critical Introduction",

> "... If web home pages were sites of self-presentation or identity construction through the bricolage of interests, images and links, then personal blogs and social network profiles could be seen to add an ongoing identity performance both individually and collectively, driven by Web 2.0 technologies of multimedia, content management, network building and persistent communication".[9]

Social images or the image that one presents to the public becomes very important to the youth, especially those in their teen years, as acceptance amongst their peer groups and especially amongst close friends seems to be of paramount importance to young people, much more than what their parents or elders think of them.

Table 3 Summary of social media popularity findings

		What social media platforms do you use?	According to you, which social media type is widely used in Kenya?	Which social media platforms do you use the most?	Which is your favourite social media platform
1	Facebook	56.52%	52.17%	27.54%	24.53%
2	whatsApp	59.42%	52.17%	49.28%	45.28%
3	Youtube	50.72%	20.29%	13.04%	
4	Instagram	23.19%	14.49%	2.90%	0%
5	Twitter	39.13%	26.09%	11.59%	9.43%
6	Google +	34.78%	1.45%	5.80%	1.89%
7	Others	7.25%	0%	N/A	3.77%

Fig 4.2 Summary of social media popularity findings

> "Social technology tools provide individuals the opportunity to create a profile space and identity that expresses their self-image (boyd, 2007a). Individuals take pictures and compose messages on their cell phones and laptop computers and thereby express themselves". [10]

Teenagers try hard to conform to the peer culture environment, and when siblings or parents step into this protected area, then things can get awkward. Many teens lead high individual personalised and self-protected lives, and put up a bold front even when all around them, the bastions of everything that they regard as important, are crumbling. The picture gets complicated if say the mother of her teen, rebellious son, wants "in" into her son's Facebook page. His deeds will be exposed to the wrong social group; and then, rather than try and reform himself he may well retreat into a socially distant cocoon from which it is difficult or even perhaps impossible to emerge. And however much parents may look down, condemn or even bar such activities, at the transient age of the threshold at which teenagers live, such activities are essential.

> "Through such activities, teenagers compare identities (Barker, 2009), which is a socialization process at work as it reflects the physical, face-to-face school culture. As with this culture, social network environments teach individuals self-control (i.e., what to post/what not to post), tolerance (i.e., accepting others' posts), and respect for one another. This environment also allows them the

> opportunity to view multiple perspectives on things, and to learn how to express themselves in a healthy manner (Hinduja & Patchin, 2009)". (Ibid)

Perhaps one of the biggest advantages of social media sites is that there is no starting or shutting down of communication. The channels for texting, messaging, calling or conferencing are open 24x7, and so teens and youth can chat, message, share jokes, vital information or even bully someone else at a time which suits them. Also, in the case of close friends or lovers, these channels allow them to stay virtually close to each other even if they are on different continents. Expressions of sexuality, views on Gender and many such related issues which figure prominently in the lives of teens, are also better addressed through communication on social media channels.

> "sociologists find that girls between thirteen and fifteen use social media, chat rooms, and role-playing games to switch genders, express emotions that feel taboo offline (such as sexual desire and aggression), and challenge norms around acting feminine. Teenage girls even go online to push back against sexual harassment and sexist behavior".

4.4 Role of Government and Governmental bodies

The roots of government involvement in surveillance can be traced back to historical contexts where rulers sought to maintain control and quell dissent.

However, the advent of the digital era has drastically transformed the nature and scope of surveillance. Governments now harness advanced technologies to monitor citizens, ostensibly to combat terrorism, crime, and other threats to national security.

But this could also include surveillance and monitoring of the netizen's activity and poses a serious threat to personal privacy The evolution of surveillance practices raises pressing questions about the extent of government authority and the potential erosion of personal privacy.

National Security Imperatives

One of the primary justifications for government involvement in data surveillance is the need to ensure national security. In an interconnected world, where information can be disseminated globally within seconds, governments face unprecedented challenges in preventing and responding to security threats. Surveillance measures, including the monitoring of digital communications and data collection, are seen as essential tools for identifying and mitigating potential risks.

The rise of cyber threats, transnational crime, and terrorism has provided justification for robust surveillance systems being installed to safeguard the well-being of citizens. Governments argue that access to extensive datasets allows them to identify patterns, predict potential threats, and respond swiftly to emerging crises. As in the case of Dataminr which arose after the attack on the Boston Marathon. The use of data surveillance in counterterrorism efforts has become a cornerstone of national security strategies in many countries.

4.5   Privacy Concerns and Civil Liberties

While national security is of paramount concern, the growing reach of government surveillance has sparked significant concerns about the erosion of privacy rights and civil liberties. Critics argue that the indiscriminate collection and analysis of personal data pose a threat to individual freedoms, as citizens may feel constantly under scrutiny by the very entities entrusted with their protection.

Mass surveillance programs, such as those revealed by whistleblowers like Edward Snowden, have highlighted the extent to which governments can access and analyze vast amounts of personal information (BigData) without proper oversight or even reason. The tension between privacy and security intensifies as governments expand their surveillance capabilities, often without clear legal frameworks or adequate checks and balances.

4.6   Future of Private and Public Spaces

It appears that the erosion of personal space, privacy and domestic internet security is going to be slowly eroded as we push forward in the inexorable march towards so called technological progress. Many science fiction films which portray the invasion of the "Big Brother" into the homes of people, the constant surveillance through the use of bots, sophisticated algorithms and cookies which one has to forcibly accept when one is navigating the net, is now fast becoming a tragic reality. As long as we continue to use the Internet (and in today's day and age, this is an inescapable fact) there will be multifarious ways of monitoring, tracking and updating both confidential and non-confidential information as Big Data seems to become the biggest need of the hour. What began as a seemingly harmless tool to enhance marketing strategies has now expanded to mining and surveillance activities that encompass all spheres of human activities and endeavours. The thin bubble that separated personal space from public space, from private activities to community gestures, has burst and the complete transparency that has erupted as a result to which the new millennium is now subject too, has threatening visions of a dystopian future grimly awaiting us.

References

[1] Rohlinger, D. A. (2019). *New media and society*. New York university press.

[2] Skogerbø, E., & Krumsvik, A. H. (2015). Newspapers, Facebook and Twitter: Intermedial agenda setting in local election campaigns. *Journalism Practice*, *9*(3), 350-366.

[3] Roberts, J. (2019). The erosion of ethics: From citizen journalism to social media. *Journal of Information, Communication and Ethics in Society*, *17*(4), 409–421. https://doi.org/10.1108/JICES-01-2019-0014

[4] Kaya, T., & Bicen, H. (2016). *The effects of social media on students' behaviors; Facebook as a case study*. Computers in Human Behavior, 59, 374–379. https://doi.org/10.1016/j.chb.2016.02.036

[5] Clark, J. R. (2010). Social media and privacy. *Air medical journal*, *29*(3), 104107.

[6] Mooney, C. (2015). *Online privacy and social media*. ReferencePoint Press.

[7] Hoffmann, C. R., & Bublitz, W. (Eds.). (2017). Pragmatics of social media. De Gruyter Mouton.

[8] Walsh, J. P., & O'Connor, C. (2019). Social media and policing: A review of recent research. Sociology compass, 13(1), e12648.

[9] Lister, M., Dovey, J., Giddings, S., Grant, I., & Kelly, K. (2008). New media: A critical introduction. Routledge.

[10] Weber, N. L. (2014). *Cyberbullying: Causes, consequences, and coping strategies*. LFB Scholarly Publishing LLC.

CHAPTER FIVE

Security at the crossroads; Invasion of personal spaces, cyber frauds, cyber bullying and harassment

5.1 Introduction

Have you ever noticed that whenever you are browsing through any website, especially those related to products, very soon after some hours, advertisements (ads) related to the product you were looking for pop up in other web pages that you surf through, even if those pages are completely unrelated to the product that you were first interested in. The same happens with movies. Watch a couple of genre specific films, say for example "Wild West" films and the very next day, movies of a similar genre appear when you log into Youtube next. What is happening here? Small little tracker objects called "cookies" are tracking every move you make, every mouse click, which target area are your eyeballs resting on, and all the images or text that you click on. These are meticulously analysed by Google and ads related to the product that you might have casually surfed by, will begin to surface, often with annoying and insistent regularity. This Orwellian feeling of being watched by your "big brother", of being under digital scrutiny continuously, where all your mouse clicks and highlights are being tracked, has led to increasing suspicion of net usage in recent times and some have even taken the extreme step of avoiding surfing for a few days or even months, in the vain hope that somehow the persistent Google monitoring system might go away, fade, over time. But even more serious than this loss of personal space and privacy, is the phenomena of cyber bullying and harassment that has emerged in recent times.

5.2 Cyber harassment and Cyber bullying

Although a relatively recent phenomena, this malaise is permeating into the lives of teens and pre-teens at an alarmingly rapid rate. Bullying as a form of power assertion probably existed ever since the inception of schools. Although the forms and strategies adopted between actual (physical) bullying and bullying on the net are different, there are many similarities. The act of bullying usually takes place between people of the same age group and/or school grade. Although bullying or ragging as it is sometimes known, may be inflicted by a senior on a junior (or vice versa, although such instances are very rare), it often occurs, that a student in a class is harassed, sometimes even to the point of suicide, by another student in the same class or grade. While this is usually the case, this is in no way a norm or a *"fait accompli"*. Young teens can be bullied even by someone as important as the President of the United

States as was quoted in "VICE News" on the web, by an eye-catching clickbait headline.

> "Donald Trump, president of the United States and husband of anti-cyber-bullying crusader Melania Trump, spent his Thursday morning cyber-bullying a teenage girl".[1]

This time, his signature Twitter ire was directed at Greta Thunberg, the teen climate activist named as TIME Magazine's annual "Person of the Year" Wednesday. Her crime? Being young and indignant about climate change!

5.3 The Nature of Cyberbullying

Most of the time, a bully is usually a person who is larger and physically more powerful than the one whom s/he has chosen as a target. Studies at different points in time have shown that boys are normally more exposed to indirect forms of bullying than girls.

> "By indirect we mean that the bully influences others to commit direct forms of aggressive worrying behaviour rather than allowing himself to take responsibility on himself".[2]

Although cross bullying does occur where a male aggressor may constantly provoke or harass a female victim, incidences of this kind are fewer than bullying which takes place between people of the same sex. Nansel et al. (2001) found that boys were more likely to be both perpetrators and victims. Other studies have found that the size of a class or domicile (whether the victim resides in an urban or rural home) has relatively little impact on the frequency of occurrence of bullying. (Olweus, 1993, Seals & Young, 2003).

Bullying is somewhat omnipresent and is unrelated to differences in class, gender, age or race. If there can be one redeeming feature stated of bullying is that it has so far, been completely unbiased!

While this phenomenon has been growing in recent years and is a noteworthy cause of concern amongst parents and relatives of victims, it is not as though as though the victim is so hapless or so totally neglected as is often portrayed by the media. Says noted author, media critic and ex NDTV bureau editor, Jyothsna Mohan Bhargava in her book

"Stoned, Shamed and Depressed",

> "...but a stalker is not lurking at every corner nor is a bully ready to pounce at every turn. And even among those who have encountered such things, there are also stories of fightbacks: teen victims of ragging have come back to use the same medium to raise a voice against the bullies; victims of sexual assault have shared their powerful stories of survival. The distinction is in being strong enough – and old enough – to harness the good of the internet while circumventing the more tempting bad. Many would perhaps agree that in 2019 it was not Kylie Jenner but Greta Thunberg who became the social media sensation".[3]

When and where do these acts of bullying take place? It is fairly self-evident that in the case of cyberbullying, since the phenomena is a product of activities in digital spaces, time and locations are of no consequence. However, in the case of actual bullying, mostly the kind of bullying that takes place in schools and colleges, studies have shown that a high percentage takes place in class itself, particularly within the supposedly hallowed precincts of esteemed high schools.

The following table shows the timings when usually bullying takes place as well as the frequency.[4]

No.	Where	Percentage
1	During Class	77% 78%
2	During Lunch	83% 75%
3	During School Events	63% 66%
4	Recess	61%
5	Class Breaks	46%
6	On the Way to School	34% 27%
7	On the Way Home from School	62%

Table 5.1. Where Bullying Takes Place

Shifting the focus from physical bullying to bullying in the cyber domain, recording and making predictions become a little more complex on account of a lack of a suitable definition of what exactly constitutes cyberbullying. A chance or a careless remark on a social media site like Facebook maybe just that. A chance remark. But very often the media exaggerates this remark to a scale where it enters the area of cyberbullying. Different scholars have at different points of time based on their research which may be area or time specific, have come with their own definitions or constructs on when an act can be regarded as cyberbullying. It is generally acknowledged that Cyberbullying can be defined as an[5],

> "aggressive, intentional act carried out by a group or an individual, using electronic forms of contact, repeatedly and over time against a victim who cannot easily defend him or herself"

Patchin and Hinduja who have conducted extensive studies on this subject broadly define cyberbullying as "bullying via an electronic medium (Li, 2006; Patchin & Hinduja, 2006). But the picture painted here is on an extremely vast canvas, and can lend itself to a lot of confusion, as forms of cyberbullying vary depending on the medium or the technology that is used. Thus, for example, bullying on Facebook or Twitter may be very different from what is more commonly resorted to on WhatsApp because of format and technical restrictions. Through email or instant messaging, numerous fake identities can be constructed but this becomes more difficult, when using social media sites like Instagram or Facebook. In recent years, this highly irregular practice has increased in its nefarious notoriety.

A survey conducted in 2007 revealed that 43% of teens out of 832 teenagers had undergone some form of cyberbullying (Moessner, 2007). According to Juvonen and Gross (2008) 72% of respondents reported at least one online incident of bullying.

It appears that the most common forms of cyberbullying take place in the dark recesses of the digital domain, through chatrooms, emails, instant messaging services such as WhatsApp, Telegram etc. Studies have shown that in at least 60% of the cases, the results of bullying have been ignored,

> "...50% said they were disrespected by others, 30% have been called names, 21.4% have been threatened by others, 19.8% were annoyed by others, 19 3% were made fun of by others, and 18.8% had rumours spread about them." [6]

No	Cyberbullying Statistics	Percentage
1	Percent of students who report being cyber bullied	52%
2	Percent of teens who have experienced cyber threats online	33%
3	Percent of teens who have been bullied repeatedly through their mobile phones or the internet	25%
4	Percent of teens who do not tell their parents when cyberbullying occurs	52%
5	Percent of teens who have had embarrassing or damaging pictures taken of themselves without permission	11%

Table 5.2. Experience of Cyberbullying

In incidences of cyberbullying usually there are four categories of perpetrators and victims together involved. Thus, there is the perpetrator, the victim, the non-involved and the bully victim. (Kowalski, Limber, & Agatston, 2012; Olweus, 1993; Wong, Chan, & Cheng, 2014).

Strangely, but in cyberbullying the prevalence rate for cyberbullies who are also victims of cyberbullying themselves is much higher. There is strong evidence to infer that in many cases the bully-victim role is the majority group in comparison to the perpetrator and victim groups (Brack & Caltabiano, 2014).

While cyberbullying is certainly a menace that needs to be discouraged and penalised, even more serious is the cybercrime of cyber-stalking. It is of a more serious nature than generic instances of cyberbullying since while the former may be for a short duration, and may not have such serious consequences, cyber stalking on the other hand can persist for a long duration and results in much more serious and severe psychological consequences than simple cyberbullying.

Studies have indicated that nearly 90% of stalking tends to be of a sexual nature. In fact this has become so common, that a term has been specifically coined for this known as "sexting". Those who under this peculiar form of new media attack, may receive occasional or even be inundated by a stream of this messages from an unknown digital assailant or sender.

Cyber stalking in India as well as in other countries is now recognised as a serious crime punishable by law. According to the Information Technology Act of 2000,

> "If any person is publishing or sending any salacious material in the form of electronic media is to be charged under section 67 of the Act. This dose not involves the determination of the extent of liability of ISP (internet service providers) and their directors."[7]

But despite this, there hardly seems to be any kind of abatement or change in the nature of this crime. In fact, incidences only seem to be on the increase.

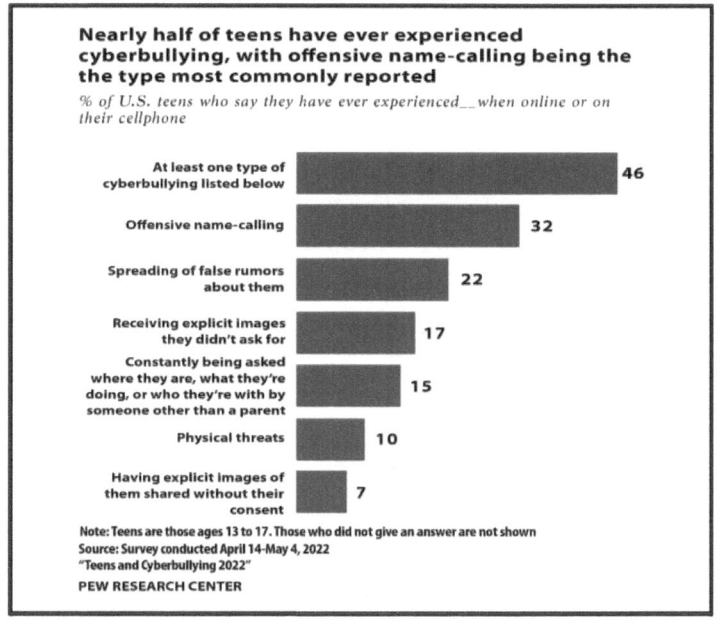

Fig 5.1. Teenage Experience of Cyberbullying

This survey shown above was conducted in the US and clearly shows that nearly half of the teen population have experienced some sort of cyberbullying. It appears that in India, the incidences of Cyberbullying are less (33% all across India), but there is full potential for this to grow and diversify in its scope. It has been observed that cyberbullying has progressed from causal remarks and occasional bullying to the extent where it finds a slot in the annals of cyber-crime, but what are some of the factors that give rise to these deplorable acts of subversive and hidden harassment? The very fact that it is often hard to detect the aggressor and trace the source from where these threats and nasty remarks originate, is what gives the bully or attacker the sense of dominance and security. S/he seems to derive comfort from the fact that he or she cannot be traced, and hence they are safe from the vantage point from which they discharge their cyber darts, somewhat akin to the feeling of security the sniper on the rooftop gets in that he feels is far from danger, and should danger or opposition approach, there is ample time to sneak away.

We have seen enough of incidences of this crime to realise its seriousness and the fact that it needs redressal. There was a time when this unique variant of cybercrimes was regarded as mere nuisance or a chance phenomenon and not really regarded as a crime. Not anymore. Now it is treated with the seriousness that it merits and at present there are legal avenues to seek redressal and justice. But what causes these bizarre and perverse events to happen in the first place? A US based report says that,

> About one-in-ten teens say they were targeted because of their gender (10%) or their race or ethnicity (9%). Teens less commonly report being harassed for their sexual orientation or their political views – just 5% each.[8]

Some are also harassed because of their physical appearance or personality although this is a lot less common. Sexual orientation plays a big role when it comes to cyber harassment. Nearly one out of ten teens cite their sexual orientation or their views on it as the reason why they are hounded, and a few (11%) feel that they were targeted because of their political views. This is much more common in Islamic countries than in non-Islamic ones as political and religious views are regarded very seriously in such countries and can often result in a deathly fate.

The gender factor also comes into play in a big way when it comes to cyberbullying. On an average, teen girls are more likely to face cyber harassment than boys (PEW, 2022). The age group of girls who are likely to face the maximum harassment, stalking and other forms of cybercrime are in the age group 15-17. This is possibly because they spend so much time on their mobile phones and also, they are most concerned about their self-image and their image vis-a-vis their peer group in this particular age bracket. In India this is not applicable but in the US many studies have been done on what role racial differences and culture plays, and it has been found that,

> "White, Black and Hispanic teens do not statistically differ in having ever been harassed online, but specific types of online attacks are more prevalent among certain groups. For example, White teens are more likely to report being targeted by false rumors than Black teens. Hispanic teens are more likely than White or Black teens to say they have been asked constantly where they are, what they're doing or who they're with by someone other than a parent." (Vogels, 2022)

Older teen girls more likely than younger girls or boys of any age to have faced false rumor spreading, constant monitoring online, as well as cyberbullying overall

% of U.S. teens who say they have ever experienced ___ when online or on their cellphone

	Offensive name-calling	Spreading of false rumors about them	Receiving explicit images they didn't ask for	Constantly being asked where they are, what they're doing, or who they're with by someone other than a parent	Physical threats	Having explicit images of them shared without their consent	Any cyberbullying
U.S. teens	32	22	17	15	10	7	46
Boys	31	16	15	13	10	5	43
Girls	32	29	19	17	10	8	49
White	35	24	16	14		6	48
Black	29	17	21	9	11	10	40
Hispanic	29	21	19	21	10	7	47
Ages 13-14	29	20	11	12	10	4	42
15-17	34	24	22	17	10	8	49
Boys 13-14	31	15	11	12	10	3	41
15-17	32	16	18	13	10	7	44
Girls 13-14	25	24	10	12	9	5	41
15-17	36	33	25	20	10	9	54

Note: Teens are those ages 13 to 17. While and Black teens include those who report being only one race and are not Hispanic. Hispanic teens are of any race. Those who did not give an answer are not shown
Source: Survey conducted April 14-May 4, 2022
"Teens and Cyberbullying 2022
PEW RESEARCH CENTER

Fig 5.2. Cyberbullying Experience
Differentiated by Gender
Source: Pew Research Centre

5.4 Effects of Cyberbullying and Cyberharrasment

Enough evidence has been gathered so far about incidences of cyberbullying, the age group and races which are most likely to face this form of harassment peculiar to the digital age. But is it so important a matter to merit so much global concern. Perhaps the biggest danger of cyber harassment is that similar to some medical diseases like Diabetes, for instance, this in a similar fashion unleashes its destructive force - internally. Unlike traditional bullying in earlier times, which often manifested itself in physical violence, sometimes leaving ugly marks, even scars on the victim, in the case of cyberbullying, the scars are psychological. And like physical scars, sometimes the damage may last a lifetime or at least take many years to heal. Often, only with the help of a good trained counsellors or psychiatrists familiar with this malaise. Social alienation, depression, self-harm, neurotic or psychotic tendencies are only some of the psychic manifestations. In extreme situations, especially when it affects your sensitive teenagers, can even lead to suicide. The table below gives one time indication of the nature of mental unease and illness that can result from prolonged exposure to this type of enervating harassment.

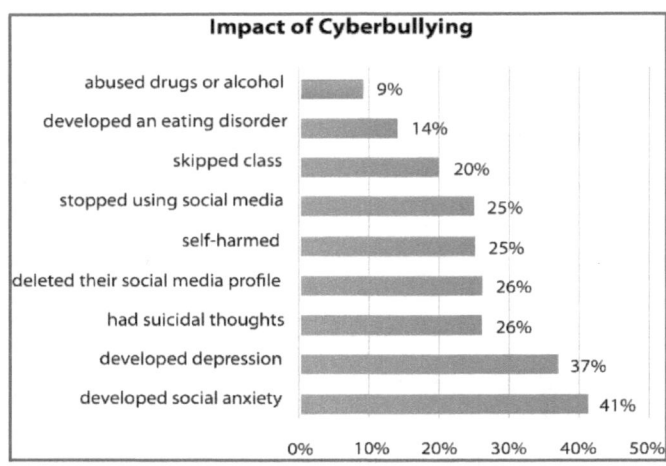

Fig 5.3. Impact of Cyberbullying

Perhaps the most disconcerting effects of cyberbullying is that it leaves lingering effects on the victim. Many of them tend to form addictive behaviours, many veer towards pornography as a form of release and almost all suffer severe blows to their self-image. Depression is a common offshoot of this peculiar form of bullying and many of them tend to stay away from school, so that they don't have to face the ones taunting and ragging them, and some even turn to alcohol as a form of respite from their misery. Researchers have found that,

> "...Both bullying and being victimized by bullying have adverse impacts on participation in risky behaviours, as both tend to be more likely to drink alcohol, smoke or chew tobacco, and take illegal substances (Berthold & Hoover, 2000; Boynton-Jarrett et al., 2008). "[9]

Some of these disorienting effects are only short term, but others last a lifetime. Children and students become disconnected with the world around them, with reality and as their self-image and self-esteem declines, they tend to withdraw into a shell. Their poor communication skills or non-existent communication skills become a serious roadblock to developing new friends and acquaintances or maintaining past relationships and the vicious cycle of lowered self-image leading to increased social withdrawal leading to even fewer friends and poor peer group image sets in. The child goes into a depression cycle and more often than not, cannot emerge out of this loop without the help of counselling or maybe even clinical psychiatry.

> "Cyberbullying produces increased feelings of social anxiety and lowered self-esteem, characteristics which can have large impacts on youth and how they interact with the world (Dempsey, Sulkowski, Nichols, & Storch, 2009; Juvonen & Gross, 2008; Mason, 2008; Willard, 2006)."

While suicide is of course regarded as an extreme measure, incidences of self-harm are more commonly found. It is almost as though the victim by inflicting harm on himself or herself is in some strange way, hurting the bully rather than hurting himself.

This can result in serious consequences and leave not just psychological but physical scars as well. (Deschamps & McNutt 2016).[10]

A study by Raskauskas and Stoltz (2007) revealed that nearly all cyberbullying victims are severely maladjusted in society. 31% of victimised students reported being very or extremely upset, 19% were very or extremely scared and 18% were very or extremely embarrassed by online harassment.

Perhaps the worst of the consequences is the feeling of social alienation. The feeling the teen gets that "no one understands him/ her". Says one student,[11]

> "People were saying stuff behind my back. Like I was a bad friend and other inappropriate names... through MySpace. It made me feel angry and depressed because if I was being a bad friend then why did they even bother to talk to me? I stopped talking to them and changed schools.[12]

Victims of this persistent form of bullying are thus affected in three important social strata - the home, the school and the friend's circle. Consistent and constant sympathetic support from home can help alleviate the problem but it still remains as children in their teen years tend to display rebellious behaviour and depend more on help and support from their friends and others within their circle of friends rather than going to their siblings or even worse still to their parents, whom the cyber victim feels, are too old and old fashioned to understand what is going on inside the traumatised victim's head.

Conclusion

We have seen that there is not one, but multiple problems related to serious victims of cyberbullying, cyber harassment and stalking. But what remedial steps are the netizens of our country taking to rectify or resolve the problem? What about the governmental agencies and the Government themselves? Are there avenues for legal addressal?

Perhaps the biggest problem with this particular malaise is that the victim retreats into a shell, refuses to divulge and share, even with select peers, his or her problem. In fact, the victim usually feels that it is of no concern to anyone except himself or herself. In such a situation it is near impossible to help the victim because they don't usually seek out help. The only time they an actually be helped is when they recognise that they are in fact, actually "victims" of cyberbullying, and if they raise their voices then forums, legal or otherwise, do exist that can come to their aid.

In India, although certainly this problem is not of the same gargantuan proportions as it is in the US, nevertheless the Indian law does provide succour to the victim(s) and stringent measures against the offender.

> "In order to guarantee legal identity for the electronic interchange of data, the IT Act of 2006 came into effect. Up to three to five years in jail and a fine of

> one lakh rupees, or both, may be imposed for computer-related offences, and in extreme circumstances, even more. Sections 66A, 66C, 66D, and 66E of the IT Act impose penalties on anybody found guilty of an offence involving disrespectful behaviour online, on social media, or with other digital media. IT Act sections 67, 67A, and 67B address the publication and electronic transmission of content involving sexually explicit acts, etc".[13]

There are several sections of the Indian Penal Code that deal with this issue. Specifically, Section 354A deals with harassment, Section 292A with blackmailing and section 354D with stalking. In addition to that to protect minors and children from different forms of sexual abuse including abuse through the cyber medium, the POCSO Act (Protection of Children from Sexual Offences) was set up in 2012 and was initiated to deal with the triple crimes of sexual assault, sexual harassment and pornography. The 'Nirbhaya funds scheme' also was initiated, which offers to ensure safety for women and children.

Cyberbullying and cyber harassment is now no longer recognised as an occasional act of malice or an avenue to air a grievance. It is now legally and socially considered a crime worthy of taking note and resolving, and avenues for justice and social reform are now freely (or in paid form) available. But regardless of how many counsellors and psychologists are there to provide hope and sympathy, despite the concerns of agitated parents and the legal system which does provide laws (although the efficacy of these laws, and how speedily justice is secured is debatable), ultimately societal reform is the answer. People, particularly students need to be re-educated, they need to realise the seriousness of their verbal and non-verbal cyber assaults and realise that their trajectory of behaviour can land their classmate, maybe even a distant friend into a cesspool of irreversible actions that can lead to serious mental trauma, sickness, and in worst circumstances, even death. It is time that awareness of this new media cybercrime is escalated and receives the attention it so richly deserves, so that remedial action can be taken. And speedily implemented so that we can live in a state that is truly a welfare state and where the needs of the individual as well as the body politic are served and satisfied to the betterment of all.

References

Trump, Being Best, Just Bullied Greta Thunberg on Twitter. (n.d.).

Retrieved November 11, 2023, from
https://www.vice.com/en/article/8844mz/trump-being-best-just-bullied-greta-thunberg-on-twitter

[2] Trump, Being Best, Just Bullied Greta Thunberg on Twitter. (n.d.).

Retrieved November 11, 2023, from
https://www.vice.com/en/article/ 8844mz/trump-being-best-just-bullied-greta-thunberg-on-twitter

[3] How Common Is Cyberbullying Among Adults? Exploring Gender, Ethnic, and Age Differences in the Prevalence of Cyberbullying—PubMed. (n.d.).

Retrieved November 11, 2023, from https://pubmed.ncbi.nlm.nih.gov/ 31697598/

[4] Bhargava, J. M. (2020). Stoned, Shamed, Depressed: An Explosive Account of the Secret Lives of India's Teens. India: HarperCollins.

[5] Weber, N. L. (2014). Cyberbullying: Causes, consequences, and coping strategies. LFB Scholarly Publishing LLC

[6] Dooley, J. J., Pyżalski, J., & Cross, D. (2009). Cyberbullying Versus Face-to-Face Bullying: A Theoretical and Conceptual Review. *Zeitschrift Für Psychologie / Journal of Psychology*, *217*(4), 182–188. https://doi.org/10.1027/0044-3409.217.4.182

[7] Kiriakidis, S. P., & Kavoura, A. (2010). Cyberbullying: A review of the literature on harassment through the internet and other electronic means. *Family and community health*, 82-93.

[8] *Cyber stalking in India*. (n.d.). Retrieved November 1, 2023, from https://www.legalserviceindia.com/legal/article-1048-cyber-stalking-inindia.html

[9] Vats, D. A. (2023). The Growing Threat of Cyberbullying in India. 11(4).

[10] Teens and Cyberbullying 2022 | Pew Research Centre. (n.d.). Retrieved November 12, 2023, from https://www.pewresearch.org/internet/2022/12/15/teens-and-cyberbullying2022/

[11] Weber, N. L. (2014). Cyberbullying: Causes, consequences, and coping strategies. LFB Scholarly Publishing LLC.

[12] Farhangpour, P., Maluleke, C., & Mutshaeni, H. N. (2019). Emotional and academic effects of cyberbullying on students in a

rural high school in the Limpopo province, South Africa. *SA Journal of Information Management*, *21*(1). https://doi.org/10.4102/sajim.v21i1.925)

[13] Johnson, J. M. (2009, March). The impact of cyber bullying: A new type of relational aggression. In American Counselling Association Annual Conference and Exposition (pp. 19-23).

CHAPTER SIX

Rise of Consumerism, Digital Marketing and Click bait Consumerism

The "customer is king", goes the old adage. But how relevant is this observation in the current scenario? In these days of hi-tech digital marketing, Google analytics and rampant consumerism, it appears that the customer is more of a puppet in the hands of Big Data and e-commerce manipulators rather than a powerful potentate who is authoritatively taking all the important decisions as far as commerce is concerned. In today's market driven digital domains, E-commerce, E-marketing, Telemarketing, the big home delivery giants like Amazon, Flipkart and Myntra are seemingly guiding all buying decisions from small household items to big commercial wholesale purchases. Buying and selling on digital space, navigating mega portals in the hope of fulfilling artificially created wants (not needs), is now the new normal.

6.1 Factors contributing to the rise in consumerism

Although it is fairly evident that there is much hype about globalisation, that really is the key to the escalating pace of consumerism across all market segments. The overall wealth in capital and capital accumulation, transnational flows of goods and services and increased speculation and investment, have all contributed to a general increase in the dollar or euro or rupee consumer spend across the continents. Although not all nations are developed or welfare economies, the general increase in wealth and increased desires for products, goods and services, have contributed to increased consumerism. Sellers, wholesale and retail and ecommerce outlets seizing this opportunity to maximise profits are now employing every level of marketing strategies to expand and consolidate their markets. Globalisation has not only affected market ebbs and flows and increased competition at all levels, it has also increased the pressure faced by banks and large corporations to find any kind of support to reduce their tax burden and lift regulatory constraints, so that they can match their global rivals.

According to Bagdikian (2004) and Curran (2003) the key trends were emergence of global conglomerations; Horizontal and Vertical integration and diversification, synergy and technological convergence.

6.2   Elements of Digital Marketing

As digital marketing grows in reach and influence, it is important first of all to understand what exactly is it?

Digital marketing otherwise known as online marketing is the promotion and sales of various brands using digital means of communication and purchase. This is very often confused with inbound marketing which while somewhat similar is not quite the same thing. In bound marketing works on goals first, and then once they are determined the marketing strategists then look at the or tools used to narrow down on what strategies are best aimed at the target customers. Digital marketing varies slightly from this approach in that it considers how digital tools or channels can convert market prospects. Digital branding may use several platforms or conversely, concentrate all their energies on developing one platform.

Digital marketing has multiple components in its gamut. In the early days of the Internet, marketing used to mostly comprise of e-mail marketing with companies outsourcing bulk emailing work to small businesses or free lancers. Even now, email advertising does exist, but it has now for the most part become redundant as users tend to mark the mail as spam or unsubscribe to it, so the only attention the mail receives is in first time viewing. Some mailers do not have the option to unsubscribe, so then the other option is to block the mail or mark it as spam. E-mailer advertising does have some advantages, but for the most part, it is redundant, as there are other more important mails that occupy the readers attention.

Another common strategy to promote businesses is through online reputation management. Online marketers or e-commerce business houses attempt to gain favourable reviews by seeking feedback for their products. The more favourable the number of reviews, as well as the quantum, the more the sales hike up!

E-commerce received a massive boost during the time of the pandemic. Most households were forced to remain within the confines of their homes; there was more time to surf the net and browse through a large database of catalogues and brochures of products and make comparative estimates of products before purchasing them. This was perhaps the chief medium of purchasing, since apart from a few shops and malls which remained open even during the pandemic, the bulk of sales were conducted through e-commerce platforms. Online marketing received a new impetus through social media sites like Twitter, Facebook and Instagram. These sites are subject to constant surveillance by AI tools such as Google Analytics and information regarding consumer tastes and preferences are funnelled into ads that irritatingly pop up on social media sites. Marketing through social media sites known in short as SMM is now a recognised and highly utilized digital strategy for sales conversions. As researchers Mangold and Faulds put it,

"The tools and approaches for communicating with customers have changed greatly with the emergence of social media; therefore, businesses must learn how to use social media in a way that is consistent with their business plan (Mangold and Faulds 2099)".

The tools for digital marketing are now nearly as numerous as the customers who now seem to prefer this more convenient, and infinitely more variety laden form of marketing and buying. Below are the some of the most commonly used and preferred forms of new media marketing:

6.2.1 Blogs

Blogs have a proven track record of attracting all sorts of customers to websites. From casual browsers and surfers to serious web customers. Online services tools are more influencing than traditional methods of communication (Helm, Möller, Mauroner, Conrad, 2013)

There are all kinds of blogs on the net, from travel blogs to eating and restaurant tips blogs for foodies and several others. Naturally, if a surfer is motivated after viewing the blog posts to go to a particular restaurant or diner, then the purpose of the blog is served. The same is true for travel destination, which at first glance may just seem like a nice biographical story but is really selling the tourism destination in a clever and subtle way. Blogs do help in providing the casual surfer with specific information and focus on areas of interest, but they are only one of the numerous tools available for online marketing. One of the most powerful tools available for digital curators at present is Search Engine Optimisation or SEO for short.

6.2.2 Search Engine Optimisation

This is a very important web analytic tool, which uses complex algorithms to look for frequently used keywords and oft repeated phrases to come up with suggested websites and/or products that may match your possible need. It is sometimes also known as Paid Search Marketing. The website should naturally address technicalities that are related to possible content and query matching, indexing, spidering and deciphering non-text content. Within this complex mechanism there are different options to choose from. Thus, you may opt for PPC (Pay-per-Click) or CPC (cost-per-click) model. SEM is applicable on multiple platforms like Google Ad words, Bing Ads (on Yahoo Bing Network) and also includes other advertising gimmicks such as Search Retargeting and Site Remarketing. Also featured prominently are Paid Social Advertising and Mobile Marketing.

As mobile phone usage multiplies with the onset of every passing year, all technological strategies are now concentrating increasingly on the mobile market. Dushinski (2009) terms mobile marketing as a revolutionary tool for connecting companies with each of their clients. There are different strategies that companies use when mobile marketing. They may use text promos, push notifications. Further methods include in-apps or marketing through different games that actually promote products.

Mobile advertising emerged as a cornerstone of digital marketing strategies. The shift towards mobile consumption prompted marketers to invest heavily in mobile advertising to reach users where they spent most of their online time. The use of location-based services and personalized targeting became key features in mobile advertising. Marketers could leverage geolocation data to deliver targeted messages based on a user's physical location, enhancing the relevance of advertisements. This personalized approach significantly increased the effectiveness of marketing campaigns.

6.3 Social Media Dominance on Mobile

The dominance of social media on mobile devices has had a profound impact on digital marketing. Platforms like Facebook, Instagram, Twitter, and LinkedIn have become essential channels for businesses to connect with their target audience. Mobile friendly interfaces and the seamless integration of multimedia content have made social media a dynamic and engaging platform for digital marketing campaigns.

6.4 Influencer Marketing impact on Mobile Marketing

In the mobile era, influencer marketing gained prominence as a powerful strategy. Social media influencers, with their niche follower base, have now become valuable partners for brands seeking authentic and reliable promotion. Influencer marketing on mobile devices allows for direct and personal connections between brands and consumers, fostering trust and loyalty.

6.5 Mobile e-commerce and m-commerce

The rise of mobile devices has transformed the way consumers shop, giving birth to mobile commerce or m-commerce. The convenience of browsing and purchasing products through smartphones has led to a significant shift in consumer behaviour. Businesses have adapted by optimizing their websites for mobile responsiveness and developing dedicated mobile apps to streamline the shopping experience.

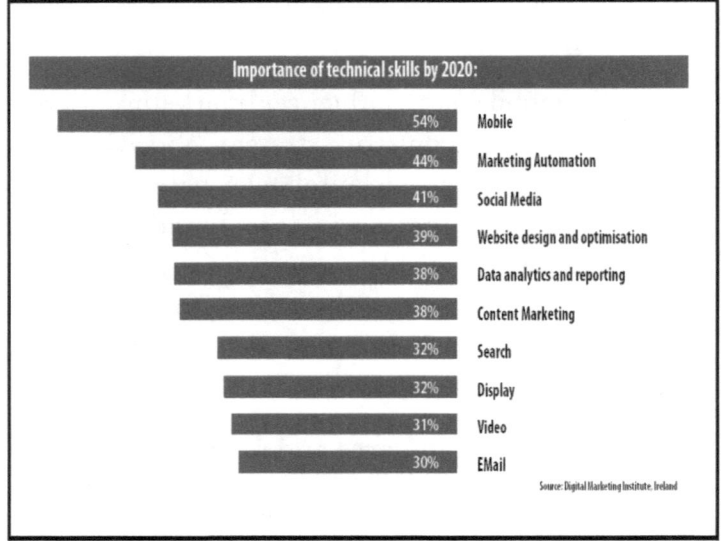

Fig 6.1: Importance of Technical Skills by 2020

Source: Digital Marketing Institute, Ireland

6.6 New Challenges and Opportunities

While mobile digital marketing offers numerous opportunities, it also presents challenges for businesses. The diversity of devices, screen sizes, and operating systems pose a real challenge for creating a consistent user experience. Adapting to the rapidly evolving technology landscape requires continuous innovation and updates to stay relevant.

Additionally, privacy concerns and the implementation of stricter regulations, such as GDPR and CCPA, have forced marketers to reconsider their data collection and targeting practices. Balancing personalized marketing with user privacy is a delicate challenge that requires a thoughtful and transparent approach.

While mobile marketing is certainly on the rise, heralded as the new advertising platform for the future and one that is here to stay, there are many other tricks up the digital marketers sleeve.

One very important aspect of digital marketing whose effect we witness every time we visit a website, but whose inner workings we are not acquainted with is Web Analytics. This is an extremely convoluted piece of software driven by complex algorithms which help collect, measure and understand browsing patterns and based on them predict which associated brands and products that you might be interested in. Do not make the mistake of confusing this with Web statistics. The latter is simply collecting and tabulating user preferences and browsing patterns, whereas Web analytics analyses, segregates and makes predictive assumptions based on big data gathered over a period of time. This is now possible after the meteoric growth of Artificial Intelligence systems which have now become an indispensable marketing tool. ANN (Artificial Neural Networks) augmented with Machine Learning and Deep Learning are all sophisticated tools put to the task of gauging short- and long-term consumer preferences.

Some important Web Analytics tools dominating the current market are Google Analytics, Spring Metrics, Woopra, Clicky, Mint and Chartbeat.

6.6.1 Click bait advertising

A very unique and a very successful form of digital marketing employed today by website developers, promoters and influencers is click bait advertising. The term is self-explanatory, but some definitions would be in order here.

The Merriam-Webster dictionary defines clickbait as

> "Something (such as a headline) which makes the users want to click on a hyperlink especially when the link leads to an item of dubious value or interest".

The Cambridge Dictionary defines it as

> "an internet story, title, image, etc. that is intended to attract attention and encourage people to click on a link"

Most of these oneliners that act as a "hook" to trap the unsuspecting web surfer, are better known as "clickbait headlines". Many people find these headlines irritating and tend to ignore it as undesirable spam

Clickbait headlines have been recognized as spam by online users (e.g., Potthast, Köpsel, Stein, & Hagen, 2016), but results indicate that clickbait headline can be perceived positively if they are created properly. Clickbait headlines appear to be an effective strategy to increase online users' arousal and curiosity.

Numerous studies have been conducted on clickbait advertising, which will be examined shortly. What is known and tangible is that they are effective in grabbing viewers' attention. So how does this work?

A large part of the success or failure of a clickbait headline on attention grabbing lies in the way the headline is framed or written. Some portions of the text are made much attractive, more eye catching or simply more sensational. It also has the same elements that movie trailers and teasers have by only making a suggestion and leaving the rest up to the viewer/reader. For example, in 2010, a media site by the name of "Upworthy" enticed the viewers by calling themselves the "fastest growing media site of all time".

> "Less than two years after it was founded in March 2012, by Eli Pariser and Peter Koechley, Upworthy had over 80 million unique visitors each month—more than the New York Times or Washington Post. In November 2013, however, Facebook announced that it would penalize deceptive headlines in their ranking algorithm, and within a year, Upworthy's business collapsed".

Although many decry the apparent "gimickyness" of clickbait headlines, not all of them can be dismissed as trivia or as mere cheap sensationalism. Sometimes, and this is more disconcerting, clickbaits directly relate to the readers fears.

There is in fact, even a connotative term just for this known as "emotional clickbait", since it relates and appeals to the emotions of the reader.

Clickbait headlines use multiple strategies to attract a viewer. One of them is a narrative strategy called "forward reference", which contains just enough information to pique the readers' curiosity. The unfortunate fact related to this unique form of advertising is that even if the viewer finds the whole concept of clickbaits as annoying,

> "they still click if the level of emotion conveyed in the clickbait headlines is extreme (Reis et al., 2015)".
>
> Many readers find clickbaits as annoying, repetitive and undesirable. And yet despite awareness of its negative aspects, still repeatedly fall prey to it. It is also, on several occasions, used by news channels to grab eyeballs.

"For example, CNNTM appears to be the top publisher that publishes news headlines written using clickbait styles to engage users on Facebook™ (Boland, 2018; Ingram, 2018). As suggested in the marketing domain, appropriately written clickbait headlines can literally appear to be legitimate and effective strategy to boost the number of website visits (e.g., Owens, 2016; Shewan, 2018)" (ibid).

6.7 Future of the digital market

Digital marketing has evolved at an unprecedented pace, transforming the way businesses connect with their audiences. As we step into the future, the landscape of digital marketing is poised for even more radical changes, driven by technological advancements, shifting consumer behaviors, and the relentless pursuit of innovation. Below are summarised some key trends that are shaping the future of digital marketing.

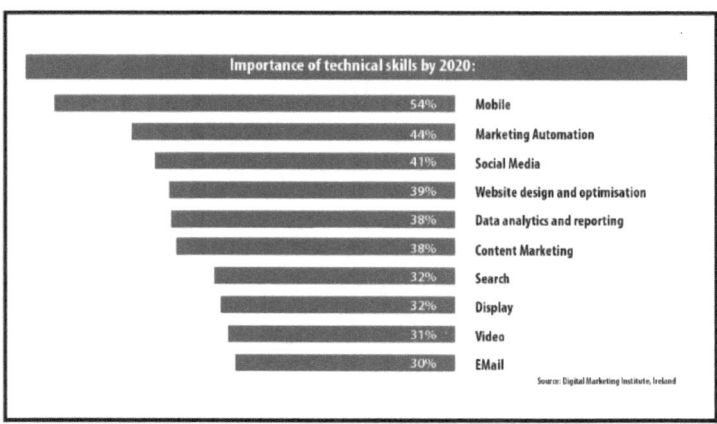

Fig 6.2: Importance of Technical Skills by 2020

Source: Digital Marketing Institute, Ireland

1. **Artificial Intelligence (AI) and Machine Learning (ML):** AI and ML are revolutionizing digital marketing by providing unprecedented

insights and enhancing personalization. Predictive analytics, chatbots, and recommendation engines powered by AI enable marketers to understand consumer behavior more accurately and deliver tailored content. Automation of routine tasks allows marketers to focus on strategy, creativity, and building meaningful relationships with their audience.

2. **Augmented Reality (AR) and Virtual Reality (VR):** The integration of AR and VR in digital marketing is creating immersive experiences for consumers. From virtual try-on experiences for products to augmented reality advertisements, these technologies are reshaping the way brands engage with their audience. As AR and VR become more accessible, marketers can anticipate increased adoption for enhancing customer interactions and driving brand loyalty.

3. **Voice Search and Conversational Marketing:** The rise of voice-activated devices and smart speakers is changing the way people search for information. Marketers need to optimize their content for voice search, as it demands more conversational and natural language. Conversational marketing, facilitated by chatbots and voice-activated assistants, allows brands to engage with customers in real-time, providing instant solutions and building stronger connections.

4. **Data Privacy and Personalization:** With growing concerns about data privacy, consumers are becoming more cautious about how their information is used. The future of digital marketing lies in striking a balance between personalized marketing efforts and respecting user privacy. Marketers must prioritize transparent data practices, offering consumers control over their information while still delivering personalized and relevant content.

5. **Video Dominance:** Video content continues to dominate the digital landscape, with platforms like YouTube, TikTok, and Instagram Reels gaining immense popularity. Short-form videos and live streaming are becoming integral components of digital marketing strategies. Brands that effectively leverage video content can capture the attention of their audience, tell compelling stories, and boost engagement.

6. **Ephemeral Content:** Ephemeral content, such as stories on platforms like Snapchat and Instagram, has become a powerful tool for marketers. The temporary nature of these posts creates a sense of urgency, encouraging immediate interaction. Marketers will increasingly focus on creating engaging and authentic ephemeral content to connect with their audience in the fleeting moments of the digital realm.

7. **Blockchain Technology:** Blockchain holds significant promise for enhancing transparency and security in digital marketing. With blockchain, marketers can ensure the authenticity of their advertisements, combat ad fraud, and create more trust in their campaigns. As concerns over digital ad fraud and data integrity persist, blockchain solutions are likely to play a crucial role in the future.

Conclusion

The future of digital marketing is an exciting and dynamic landscape, driven by technological innovations that continue to redefine the industry. As marketers navigate these changes, the key lies in embracing agility, staying abreast of emerging trends, and consistently delivering value to an increasingly discerning audience. Digital marketing will very soon prove to be the new "*sine qua non*" of the future, as more and more digital converts turn to this new avenue that holds infinite promises for quick commercial gains. Exactly to what extent are these multipronged strategies making inroads into the personal space of citizens and is constant and aggressive marketing justified, is an area which enters the domain of ethics, and is not an issue which will be dealt with in this chapter. Be that as it may, it is certainly crystal clear that digital marketing in all its numerous "avatars" is here to stay and will dominate the market for many decades in the future.

References

[1]Pengnate, S. F., Chen, J., & Young, A. (2021). Effects of Clickbait Headlines on User Responses: An Empirical Investigation. Journal of International Technology and Information Management, 30(3), 1–18. https://doi.org/10.58729/1941-6679.1440

CHAPTER SEVEN

It's all about Data!
Data Journalism, Data Analytics and Data Mining

7.1   Data Journalism

The face of Journalism has undergone a complete transformation in the last two decades. From a creative and news driven profession and career it has now mutated into a data driven highly technical profession, where technicalities and factual data drive the news rather than awareness and a "nose for news" as was the norm in the past. Partly, this is due to the advancement of technology. Also, partly, due to the aggressive inroads that Google and its associated partners are making into every sphere of economic and creative activity; and the increasing role that Google Analytics is beginning to play in our private and public lives. This chapter examines the recent phenomena of data journalism in depth, how data mining is undermining all our net based activities and the multitude of ways Google Analytics is playing a key role in the choices that we make in our day-to-day activities and transactions.

Why has Data journalism assumed such paramount importance of late? What are the factors that have contributed to it almost changing the face of journalism today? At first glance it appears that data journalism is a very recent new age phenomena, but in reality, apparently it first reared its unique face in 1821. The data was centred around the number of students who attended a school in Manchester and how much costs were incurred on these students in the school. With the progression of time, many journalists and news organisations realised that as the quantum of data was increasing, this was beyond the abilities of the computer hardware and software that existed at that time or the size of news organisations and many news organisations in the US and in Britain hired external programmers to source and validate data.

Data Journalism received a huge boost in spring 2010 when the Wikileaks war logs was exposed. The interactive piece "Afghanistan war logs: IED attacks on civilians, coalition and Afghan troops", presented hard to digest data in an easy and succinct way.

This pioneering effort at data journalism showed a map with 16,000 incidents caused by improvised explosive devices (IED) between January 4, 2004, and December 31, 2009, with data on the location of IEDs and the number of casualties.

Not only was the map interactive, but it featured a timeline of all attacks and highlights that contextualize important moments. The reader can zoom in and out to see each incident better and clicking on a particular attack shows details of the number of casualties and victims. By pressing start, all incidents appear on the map chronologically and automatically.

Wikileaks' exposé – and collaboration with established media organizations – is regarded as a landmark event in the field of data journalism since it enabled journalists to adopt new approaches to handling and analysing stories. Whether for the bold way in which the data was presented, or because of the importance of the information and its repercussions, the fact is, the episode of the "War Logs" brought data journalism into the limelight, raising this form of reporting to a newly recognised and now, much sought after level.

Although the reasons for the rapid and widespread growth of Data Journalism are many, two reasons can be cited as the most important factors contributing to this sudden and unprecedented meteoric growth. One, is the fairly obvious reason of "transparency". The other is shareability. By sharing data and not retaining it as secret, the user or the publisher of such data is sending messages to the public that s/he is open to others working on the data and drawing new conclusions from it. In the book "Data Journalism in the Global South", authors Bruce Mutsvairo,

Saba Bebawi, Eddy Borges-Rey state that,

"Clearly then, analysis—including that of data—is the hallmark of all journalistic practice. However, the romanticization of visual designs such as infographics, mappings, and animations by techno-optimists as definitive of data journalism simply misses the point about the immense contributions of data journalism to contemporary investigative reporting".[1]

Definitions of Data Journalism vary from country to country and from region to region. But most of the definitions attribute the term to Simon Rogers who first used the term in a post to the "Guardian Insider Blog". This happened way back in 2015 and since then, the parallel stream of Data Journalism has gained more ground. It now comprises of spreadsheets, Graphics, Infographics and Data Analysis.

According to Veglis and Bratsas, data journalism essentially is the,

> "Process of extracting useful information from data, writing articles based on information and embedding visualisations in articles that help readers to understand the significance of stories".[2]

Others feel that there is no essential differences between data journalism and main stream journalism. Brian Boyer of the

Chicago Tribune has commented that,

> "Data journalism only differs from verbal journalism in that it uses a "different kit". He goes on to add that "we all sniff out report and relate stories for living. It's like "photo journalism"; just swap the camera for a laptop". [3]

But the truth is that there are many fundamental differences between data journalism and traditional modes of journalism. Perhaps the one trait which stands out the most is "Interactivity". Data Journalism is inherently, by its very nature, much more interactive than print journalism. Datasets that are obtained or extracted are visualised into interactive interfaces that allow users to explore them. A study by Coddington in 2015, categorised visualisation interactivity into three forms. The first form of interactivity depicts a lower level of interaction with the content, allowing readers to first 'inspect' and then 'narrate', in the sense that a different section is highlighted. The second form of interactivity pertains to a higher form, where readers can decide to mark a certain section so that they can decide to see more or less detail. The third form provides even more interactivity in that readers can "filter" or reconfigure the data (customise) it to show multiple arrangements. Naturally, to make a dataset more interactive in unique ways demands the development of many unique additional skillsets. Now they need to be familiar with tools of web development and design, community management and reorganisation of data. As journalists all across the globe hone their skills and attempt to adapt it to this new and growing medium, data journalism is slowly but surely finding its way into newsrooms. This prodigal and maverick new entrant is gaining acceptance, and even in some channels, popularity scattering and challenging the centuries old established norms of print journalism.

One of the main reasons for newsrooms to gain comfort with data journalism is the new formats of data. Most of it is in a nonreadable format and the data very often is rife with errors, which have to be scanned, detected and then the data has to be cleaned before it can be presented to public view. The cost for this is enormous not only in financial terms but also in terms of time - garnering and processing time, all of which greatly hinder newsroom functioning where time is of a great premium. But at the same time, as has been already suggested,

> "... if news organisations decide not to build and maintain extensive data sets and create useful services on top of those data, the other players on the field will fill in the gap quickly". [4]

As more and more AI tools become available, gathering and gleaning of datasets, a formidable task thus far, will become easier and faster. And data journalism will play an increasing role in newsrooms.

News organisations see value in transparency which data journalism adds to the journalistic process. Data sets used in reporting are often published online and are therefore accessible for anybody to use. Angelica Peralta, editor of news applications at La Nacion in Argentina, describes this form of thinking thus,

"We believe that data show a lot of transparency, and if we can put our audience in contact with our data sets, that will give them more power to investigate themselves. So, we will do both things - release some articles and also put the database available to them". (Ibid)

7.2 Types of Data Journalism

Simon Rogers	Martha Kang	Martin Rosenbaum
By just the facts, data-based news stories local data telling stories analysis and background deep dive investigations	Narrate change over time start big and drill down start small and zoom out highlight contrasts explore the intersection dissect the factors profile the outliers	Measurement Proportion internal comparison external comparison change over time league tables analysis by categories Association

Table 7.1: Types of Data Journalism projects/stories proposed by others

Source: Journal of Media Critiques [MC] - Vol.3 No.11 2017

Transparency is not the only redeeming feature of data journalism. Data driven projects are cheaper than traditional marketing campaigns. Many data heavy projects go viral because of the buzz going around the data and the inferences being drawn from them.

Another feature drawing journalists to data journalism is interactivity. News organisations measure the amount of tweets on social media sites, the time spent on these stories, the extent of retweets and Instagram stories and these are computed and displayed in the form of raw data or infographics to determine how popular the stories are. Since it is easy to make comparisons and comparative analysis when dealing with quantitative data, many writers, even traditional hard core print writers are veering towards this new fact-based form of an ancient art.

There are many forms of interactivity. Jensen (1998) has classified interactivity into four distinct and clear forms. There is Transmissional interactivity, Consultational Interactivity, Conversational Interactivity and finally Registrational Interactivity. Transmissional interactivity is a little self contradicting in the sense it is one way communication, but here the user does have the freedom to choose from a continuous stream of information. Consultational interactivity is again a measure of the media's potential ability to choose but here the main difference is that information is communicated both ways. Conversational and Registrational interactivity are essentially variants of the same theme on selection of information.

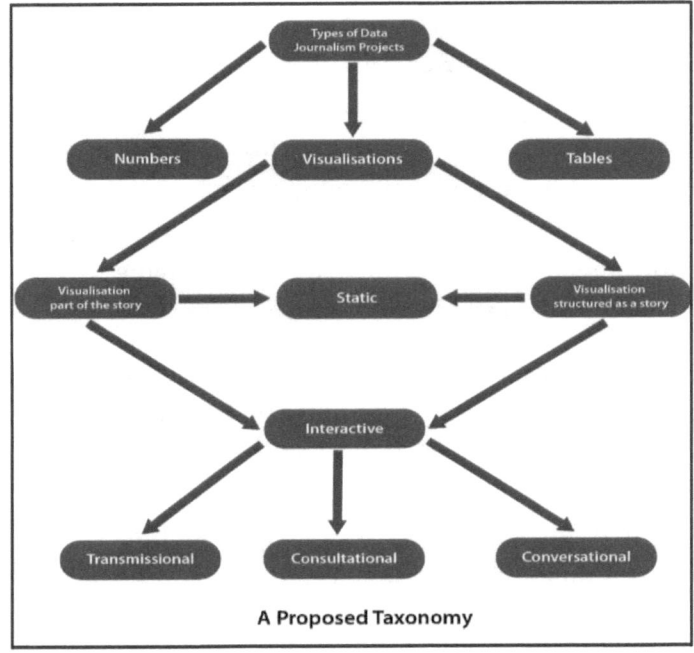

Figure 7.1 Taxonomy of Data Journalism

Source: Journal of Media (2017), pg. 116

Interactivity is a key and essential component of data journalism and a story will never be quite the same if it lacks this essential relational component.

In the study conducted on two networks which are strong examples of data journalism at work, it was found that for IndiaSpend forty-eight percent had a lower level of interaction with content that allowed the readers to see or inspect one set of data while "narrating" or showing a different section. In the case of "The Hindu", twenty-nine percent had this form of interactivity, four percent had a slightly higher form of interactivity where readers can "connect" or show related items, then if they liked it could mark it as 'interesting' and then finally abstract or elaborate in more or less detail.

So how exactly does this new form of Journalism work? Veglis and Bratsas have organised data journalism into six clearly defined stages,[5]

(1) **Data Compilation:** Compilation of data can be done in a variety of ways. It can be supplied directly by an organisation or it can be located using sophisticated scanning techniques. One can also scrape web pages to collect data, or it can be collected through the traditional methods like observations, surveys, online forms and a term which is fairly new and quite in vogue nowadays - crowd sourcing.

(2) **Data Cleaning** as its name implies, is the process of cleaning the data of all errors, and after removing glaring errors from the data convert it into a format that other journalists will understand. When doing this it is important to understand that this conversion will only be relevant and meaningful, if other journalists in the team or news network can relate to this data and are conversant with the tools, AI or non-AI, for working with large amounts of data for the conversion to be effective.

(3) The third stage is that of **Data Validation.** This is simply cross checking the data sources, cross

referencing and tracing the origins to detect whether the information is from a reliable and trusted source or not

Not only that, journalists need to dig deeper and check what was the purpose of the data generation, how, when and where it was gathered from. The more rigorous the fact-checking the more the data can be trusted and the more authentic the report of the story.

Yet another component is (4) **Data Visualisation**. This is the stage where the data literally "comes to life". When raw abstract and oft times boring data is presented through lively colourful and meaningful Infographics then not only is the data easy to decode and understand but complex relationships as well as causal relationships can be presented in an easily assimilable form so that the viewer can not only see the trees but also the overall picture, the wood containing the trees. Data visualisation here can be static visualisations like the kind we see in print (in newspapers and magazines) or it can be interactive, as in a multimedia presentation or a website. Naturally, it goes without saying that interactive multimedia presentations drive the data home much more convincingly than static data visualisations or presentations

(5) **Article Writing**. This is the last stage, but by no means the less crucial stage. This is where it all comes together. Where all the visualisations, the

interactive content and the overall content is given a shape and form. Simply garnering and presenting data without going into linkages, its significance and inter-relationships makes data journalism a dry and drab form of journalism that may appeal to only a very limited audience. While stories may be data driven, good content writing is the foundational backbone of any good story - news or non-news stories. [6]

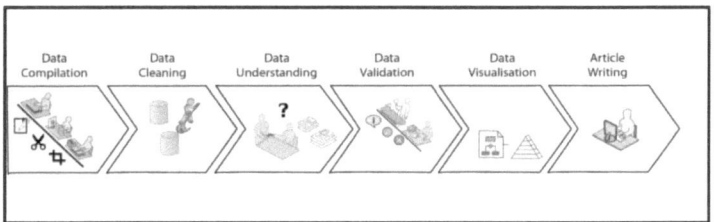

Figure 7.2 The stages of Data Journalism

Source: Veglis, A., & Bratsas, C. (2017). Towards a taxonomy of data journalism

The ways and means and techniques of data journalism have been examined at some length in this chapter. But what are the key sectors where all these new tools and techniques find application?

The first sector that comes to mind is the newsroom and news channels. In a survey conducted by the Reynolds Journalism Institute, the organisation found that much more respondents than what was envisaged were already engaged in Data Journalism projects. The new and upcoming breed of journalists see this as useful tool uncover hidden stories. In a sense, stories within stories, that otherwise would not have emerged. Not only do unique stories emerge from this kind of journalism but also, they corroborate the traditional role of news Channels and networks - and that is to serve as a "watchdog" of society. People regard this new method as something that "hits you in the face" and impacts your life more directly. As has been commented,

> "... the language of networks today is data - little points of information that are often not relevant in a single instance, but become massively important when viewed from the right angle". [7]

Data Journalism is now being used by companies to boost sales, by politicians to show how effectively their various schemes have been effective in reducing unemployment and addressing other pressing issues in the economy and also how the GDP has increased as a result of government interventions. Internationally we find that data journalism is finding increasing usage in countries as diverse as China and Africa.

In China the Caixin Media Company Ltd., a Beijing based media group, headed by veteran journalist, Shuli Hu, plan to "blaze a trail that helps traditional media prosper in the new media age through integrated multimedia platforms". A sister organisation, Caixin VisLab founded in 2013, has produced over 1000 data driven projects, winning many prestigious international awards through their pioneering and accuracy centred projects. Some of the awards they received are - "After the Flood: Never Let Bygones Be Bygones," "China's Property Market Report: A Decade of Ups and Downs," "The Explosion of Qingdao Sinopec Pipeline" and "Zhou's Power Base".

Africa, far from being left behind seems to be leading the way now in this field especially in countries like Nigeria, Rwanda and Zimbabwe. Although these countries are now waking up to the possibilities of Data Journalism, the external support that is needed is simply not prevalent. In countries like Zimbabwe, journalists bemoan the fact that revamping of journalism curriculum that is very urgent need in view of the changing face of journalism has not taken place yet, and also research institutions that can aid and abet stories with factual data are not present, nor do the authorities, academic or otherwise, see this an important criteria for quick and authenticated churning out of fact-centred stories.

As authors of the book "Data Journalism in the Global South" are quick to point out,

> "Zimbabwe therefore is still a long way in creating the overall information architecture that allows big data journalism to take root and contribute to democratic processes. Journalists in Zimbabwe therefore face a lot of challenges. This has consequences to the type of journalism that prevails in the country". (Ibid)

In Rwanda, the challenges are somewhat similar. Journalism has not developed to the extent that it should have, especially investigative journalism, and this is the field where data journalism is most needed as often cold and accurate data can validate many claims and assertions that are often made in investigative reporting of stories. The general standard of reporting seems to be sub-standard and many journalists, especially the senior ones are not trained in this particular field and see it as neither exciting nor relevant.

Taking cognisance of this upcoming need and style of reporting, the country has established the National Institute of Statistics of Rwanda (NISR) and online platforms that provide applications and online services for automated data such as ArcGIS Online (AGOL) (geospatial data).

In Nigeria, the situation seems to be somewhat better. Although here too the Government and journalists approach the subject of data journalism caution and trepidation, it is slowly gaining ground. In 2017, 25 journalists from the VOA (Voice of America) received training on the topic of tools of data journalism for the digital age.

Other concrete steps have also been taken putting Nigeria firmly on the map of applications of data journalism. On February 2018, the News Agency of Nigeria signed a Memorandum of Understanding in connection with data journalism. The Google for Elections workshop organised in Laosin 2018 was also designed to impart superior tools of data collection, analysis and interpretation, so that the accuracy superiority of data journalism could be suitably leveraged.

In many other parts of the world too, data journalism is slowly but surely, gaining ground. And acceptance. As it is tech heavy, there is a tendency for it to appeal to the younger crop of tech savvy journalists who feel a pressing need to authenticate their stories with data, so that it becomes an irrefutable document. As artificial intelligence (AI) makes increasingly makes its presence felt in every sphere of human activity, it is but natural that a tech dependent subject like data journalism will lean even more heavily on AI tools in the future. But any form of journalism, be it data driven or not, ultimately derives its success and credibility from good storytelling. And the hope of all news and non-news organisations is that data, rather than detracting from a story, should only add to it, thereby making for a well-rounded very credible form of futuristic journalism.

7.3 Google Analytics

Although Google analytics does not really fall into the purview of journalism, print, web or electronic journalism, its influence is felt so heavily in all the different avatars of journalistic writing, that it certainly deserves mention in any new media book. Whether one is surfing the net, browsing through a newspaper or writing a book even, google analytics manages to make its' presence felt.

At first glance Google Analytics appears to be a purely business tool using web based "traps" like click bait Ads and Search Engine Optimisation or SEO to enhance digital marketing methods and solutions. But Google Analytics, especially Web Analytics is now rapidly becoming the mainstay of good journalism. Web Analytics has already now threaded its way into the newsroom, and although researchers are sceptic as to what role they can possibly play, malleable and fresh minds are eager to lap up the potentialities of this new metric tool. The tools that analytics provide, the streamlining of data is innovative and nonlinear certainly, but at the same time, they also,

> "... foster profit-oriented norms and values in newsrooms by introducing web analytics as disruptive, connective and routinized in news production". [8]

What is the primary purpose of Web Analytics? According to Kaushik,

> "The entire goal of the web analytics process is to increase our desired business out- comes. We are no longer just measuring how much traffic our online business generates. We also want to measure how well it performs in business terms". [9]

What was once regarded as a high tech "nerdy" tool is now being adopted even by non-techies. It is quite literally reshaping the nature of journalism and where once such seemingly obscure and abstract data was funnelled to the so-called specialists, analytics has turned even the average "nose for news" journalist into a high performance, tech enhanced news digger. One who now combines multiple roles into one. Journalists are now reluctantly or otherwise, forced to rethink writing and news garnering styles and now,

> "… journalists are working within a newsroom culture that places, in some cases, more value on web analytics than journalistic intuition (Hanusch 2016)

There has been much hype about Google Analytics and the so called "incredible" way it has elevated online business and marketing to hitherto unforeseen levels. But what makes Google Analytics tick? Why it such a sought-after product by corporates, market houses and SMEs?

One of singularly distinguishing features of Google Analytics is that it while it is extremely reliable at tracking standard website metrics like visitors to a web page, page views, abandonment and bounce rate, it can also track business outcomes which it internally categories, as goals. Not only goals, but it can also track down different types of marketing initiatives. It can track paid searches, display advertising, social media as well as e-mail marketing.

In addition to this, it is also very adept at performing market segmentation. A small example of this is viewing the traffic on a website based on the geographical location of visitors to the site. This is achieved by a tool called "Map Overlay Report". Google Analytics not only generated hundreds of reports but it also collates and organises them in a fashion that is easy to understand and interpret as well as reproduce for consolidated report writing.

And last but not the least, Google Analytics is the go too tool for clickstream data, which it has been doing for some time. It's been over five years since it was launched, but since then, has been adopted universally by millions of small as well as large business houses.

Conclusion

The new age form of journalism is now very different from its ancestral roots. Data, authenticity and accuracy have now become the mainstay of good journalism and are now here to stay. While digital tools do have the advantage of accessibility, speed and replicability, they do sometimes take away from the "personal" people friendly touch that traditional journalists used to have with their readers and which was reflected in their writings. Google Analytics in particular, while being primarily a web-based business app is now shaking hands with Data journalism to vet and corroborate all facts and reports

This small but unique business tool has morphed from being a simple "hit collector" from websites to becoming a large and sophisticated information aggregation system that collects data from all kinds of websites - standard as well as mobile. Not only that it can also collect data from iPhone and Android apps as well as Adobe Air applications.

Data Journalism has extended its tentacles from being a first world innovation to supplementing all serious journalistic writing in the "Global South". New AI tools which greatly facilitate the creation of graphs charts and infographics make the visualisation, compilation and analysis of data so much more easier. But having said this, ultimately nothing can take away from good, accurate and well researched journalistic writing. This has always been the forte, the sword and shield of any journalist worth his calling, and always will continue to remain that way.

References

Mutsvairo, B., Bebawi, S., & Borges-Rey, E. (Eds.). (2019). *Data Journalism in the Global South*. Springer International Publishing. https://doi.org/10.1007/9783-030-25177-2

[2] Veglis, A., & Bratsas, C. (2017). Towards a taxonomy of data journalism. *Journal of Media Critiques*, *3*(11), 109-121.

[3] Michalski, D. (n.d.). *Reader Engagement with Data Journalism: Comparing the Guardian and Washington Post's Coverage of People Killed by Police*.

[4] Aitamurto, T., Sirkkunen, E., & Lehtonen, P. (2011). Trends in data journalism. *Espoo: VTT*, 0-27. (n.d.). *Journal of Media Critiques*, *3*(11)

[5] Veglis, A., & Bratsas, C. (2017). Towards a taxonomy of data journalism. *Journal of Media Critiques*, *3*(11), 109-121.

[6] Gray, J., Chambers, L., & Bounegru, L. (2012). *The data journalism handbook: How journalists can use data to improve the news.* " O'Reilly Media, Inc.".

[7] From Traditional Media to the Digital Realm [7] Belair-Gagnon, V., & Holton, A. E. (2019). The two faces of Janus: Web analytics companies and the shifting culture of news. *Journalism practice*, *13*(8), 993-997.

[8] Cutroni, J. (2010). *Google Analytics: understanding visitor behavior.* " O'Reilly Media, Inc.".

.

CHAPTER EIGHT

Digital explorations of Civic Consciousness: The Evolution of Mobile Journalism

8.1 Introduction

The journalistic content and style map is undergoing radical and phenomenal content as well as stylistic communications in recent years. While some of the old models of communication still hold good, and will continue to hold sway as long a there is a sender, a receiver and noise to scramble the intended message(s), journalism, especially broadcast journalism, is seeing a new epoch of small scale, localised, problem-specific and targeted news reporting. Broadcast journalism has stylistically and structurally moved away from the large crews, sensationalism, complex technical hardware and tech-obsessed crews to small, manageable teams who are leveraging technology only to capture news rapidly, accurately and in a time bound manner. More than hi tech gadgets, timeliness, proximity, fairness and accuracy of reporting are taking centre stage and domination of channels and largescale distribution of news through Megacorps and networks is fading away into the shadows of a bygone era. Enter the citizen journalist or the Mojo mahout who is now steering the collection, dissemination and analysis of news in an entirely new direction. Simply stated, Mobile journalism, or MoJo, refers to the practice of using mobile devices such as smartphones and tablets to capture, edit, and share news content.

8.2 The Rise of Mobile Journalism

Definitions of mobile journalism vary, ranging from precise sharply defined profiles, to nondescript, generic definitions which encompass a vast majority of techniques, both in the area of content collection and technology applications.

But nearly all of them agree that a clear distinguishing feature of mobile journalism is non-professional and non-team enabled delivery of news. Usually undertaken by a single individual who is not a journalist by profession or paid to be one, but who is simply contributing as a civic minded, socially aware and techsavvy citizen. One view cites that,

> "Citizen journalism is a term used to describe the involvement of non-professionals in the creation, analysis, and dissemination of news and information in the public interest. It has been applied variously to the activities of individual citizens sharing information on blogs, social networks, and online forums, participatory media projects organized and run by professional news organizations or civic groups, and social media users".

Most of the definitions are referring to the coverage or capture of news and news related items by amateurs, which might otherwise have been ignored for poor technical quality or other reasons but makes it to the channels and syndicated news networks by virtue of its unique peg, timeliness, frank portrayal or the multifarious reasons why some items are regarded as newsworthy and others are not. Another definition states that citizen journalism may refer to a,

> "… contribution to discussion in the public sphere, whether in the form of simple information, synthesis, reporting, or opinion. The contributions can range from very local to global, entering into the 'conversion of democracy' in media critic James Carey's phrase" (Friedland & Kim, 2009, p. 297).

All these definitions make the assumption that the news provider in question is a non-trained amateur citizen journalist who has a keen news sense, a nose for news as it were, and is willing to present his views with accuracy and as bias-free as possible. But simply because the carrier of news is untrained in the finer craftsman of filmmaking or in sound does not mean that they cannot film or cover events that no one else has captured or perhaps no one has captured with such clarity and nuance. Take for example, the images of the 2005 tsunami in Southeast Asia and the 2007 bombings of the London tube. Also, the much-viewed shooting of Oscar Grant by a BART officer in 2009. All these news capsules were celebrated for their ability to act as proxy witnesses, capturing events first-hand (Allan and Thorsen, 2009). Moyo (2011) argues that citizen journalism functions as alternative media and counter-hegemonic media.

This form of journalism that is on the increase has arisen mostly on account of technology and massive strides in the telecom industry which have made transmitting of small data, near instantaneous.

Mobile journalism has witnessed a meteoric rise in recent years, propelled by the widespread adoption of smartphones and high-speed internet connectivity.

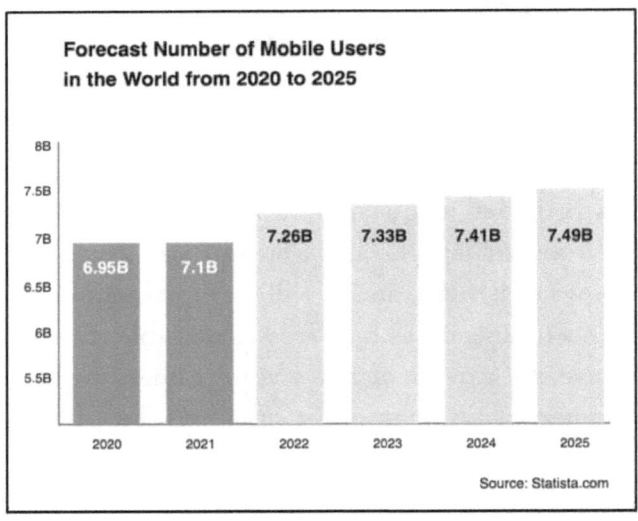

Fig. 8.1 Number of Mobile Users in the World
from 2020 to 2025
Source: Statista.com

According to a study conducted by the Reuters Institute for the Study of Journalism, 85% of news consumers access news through their smartphones, making it the primary device for news consumption globally. The portability, accessibility, and affordability of mobile devices have democratized the process of news production, enabling both professional journalists and citizen reporters to contribute to the news cycle.

According to a Pew Research Centre report, as of 2022, 85% of adults in the United States own a smartphone, with similar trends observed globally. The affordability of smartphones, coupled with the accessibility of high-speed internet, has enabled rapid access to information and news reporting tools. Information can be captured instantly and cleanly and can also be forwarded to news gathering sources with speed and alacrity.

One of the key advantages of mobile journalism is its ability to democratize news production by making it accessible to a broader range of individuals. A study published in the Journal of Communication Inquiry highlights the impact of mobile journalism in empowering marginalized communities to share their stories. Mobile devices, equipped with high-quality cameras and user-friendly editing tools, have become powerful tools for citizen journalists, allowing them to document and report on events that may otherwise go unnoticed by traditional media outlets. A study by the Tow Centre for Digital Journalism emphasizes the real-time capabilities of mobile journalism, enabling journalists to capture, edit, and publish news stories instantly. The ubiquity of the mobile phone, the instant convenience and its small footprint make it an ideal tool for quick and easy capture of news, often unnoticed. The fact that many events can be captured surreptitiously, sometimes without the consent of the party being filmed, have given rise to numerous controversies and raising an oft touted concern for ethical considerations.

8.3   Ethical Concerns

One of the primary concerns surrounding mobile journalism is the potential compromise of journalistic credibility. A study conducted by the Nieman Journalism Lab discusses the challenges of verifying user-generated content (UGC) from mobile devices, especially in situations where misinformation and fake news are prevalent. Journalists face the dilemma of balancing the need for speed with the imperative to verify the accuracy of the information they are disseminating. This study underscores the importance of developing robust verification mechanisms to maintain the trustworthiness of mobile journalism.

There is also the question that are these self-appointed semi ombudsmen qualified to take ethical and moral decisions that may seriously impact the lives of individuals who are at the centre of the coverage? In this present era of fake news, deep fakes and misrepresentation of facts, media credibility often lies in the hapless crucible of public outrage and enraged sentiment. A well-known case in point, is the record by a resident of Los Angeles, George Holliday, who somewhat managed to obtain a recording of officers beating Rodney King in 1991. Without any editing or post-processing, Holliday supplied the tape to a local news station KTLA, which aired the footage after first editing it. The video was not sufficient evidence to convict the offending officers, but it did create quite a stir in the public eye and even led to a spate of riots in Los Angeles. Another sensational Citizen journalism "ripoff" was when James O'Keefe and Hannah Miles carried out sting operations against a community organisation for reform labelled as "ACORN". The edited videos were so convincing that it resulted in US Congress eliminating its funding for ACORN, and other funders too, stopped contributing funds to this organisation. It was a potent example of the power of citizen journalism, but created a lot of venom inside the organisation inside of ACORN as well as the mainstream media prompting O'Keefe to comment that it was effectiveness that led the "mainstream news media and other elites to "curse" the citizen journalist (O'Keefe, 2013, p175).

This kind of journalism has triggered the rise of many ethical concerns regarding privacy, consent and possible "exploitation" by the amateur MoJo. The Journal of Mass Media Ethics has carried articles on the ethical considerations of capturing and sharing images or videos of individuals in distressing situations. While genuine and authentic news is most certainly welcome, the public needs the discernment to distinguish between sensational news that borders on yellow journalism and the real thing.

As technology advances and the ways and means to create "deep fake" and synthetic videos becomes increasingly facile, discernment will be a tipping point in favour of mainstream journalism versus citizen journalism. The single most important factor which has contributed a significant push to alternative media is the speed at which content can be captured and distributed. The immediacy of Mobile Journalism raises concerns about the verification and accuracy of information. A study published in the Digital Journalism journal highlighted the challenges journalists face in verifying user-generated content obtained from mobile devices. The speed at which news is disseminated through mobile platforms can compromise the traditional journalistic standards of fact-checking and verification.

8.4 Innovations in Mobile Journalism

Two fields that are reshaping the future of news reporting are

Augmented Reality (AR) and Virtual Reality (VR). Advancements in mobile technology have paved the way for immersive storytelling through augmented reality (AR) and virtual reality (VR). A study by the

Knight Foundation explores the potential of AR and VR in enhancing the audience's engagement with news content. Mobile journalists can use these technologies to create interactive and immersive narratives, providing audiences with a deeper understanding of complex issues. Authors Naz and Khan commenting from the perspective of photojournalism, believe that,

> "Augmented Reality (AR) converge productively in many visual communicational fields and generate new possible results. The future of photojournalism can also be changed via the convergence of Augmented Reality (AR) technology".

They also go on to add that in future studies, information technologies have the power to,

> "... emerge different media platforms and present new phases of communication in which foundations of mediums and sources, content and receivers are all included". (Ibid)

The advancement of virtual reality, increasing use of immersive technologies have introduced a new "reality" dimension to the encapsulation and dissemination of news especially video news, making the videos so real and convincing, that it is very hard to segregate the real from the imaginary. Advanced 3D imaging and technologies have blurred the boundaries between fake and real news, so news whether mainstream or citizen generated are becoming increasingly harder to decrypt and decipher, making them attractive to the sensation and attention seeking citizen journalist, looking for immediate reception and responses to the news s/he is putting out. Immersive storytelling approach has the potential to revolutionize the way news narratives are constructed.

Apart from advances in AR/VR technologies, bandwidth is also a major contention for attention. 4G, while fast, did place some constraints on quick capturing and dissemination of news, but these have been all but eliminated with the adoption of 5G technologies into media, which has virtually revolutionized the spread, reach and popularity of mobile journalism. A report from the International Center for Journalists (ICFJ) discusses how the increased speed and bandwidth offered by 5G networks will enable journalists to transmit high-quality, real-time content seamlessly. This development has implications for live reporting, video streaming, and the overall efficiency of mobile journalism. Social media platforms play a pivotal role in the dissemination of news generated through mobile journalism. Recent studies shed light on the symbiotic relationship between mobile journalism and social media.

A study published in the International Journal of Communication explores how social media platforms serve as essential distribution channels for mobile journalism. The instantaneous nature of social media aligns seamlessly with the real-time reporting capabilities of mobile journalism. Platforms such as Twitter, Instagram, and Facebook facilitate the rapid dissemination of news content, reaching a global audience within seconds. The study underscores the need for journalists to adapt their storytelling techniques to suit the dynamics of social media platforms.

8.5 Challenges of Misinformation on Social Media

The proliferation of news through social media also poses challenges related to misinformation and disinformation. A report by the Pew Research Centre discusses the role of social media in amplifying misinformation, particularly when news is disseminated through user-generated content from mobile devices. The study emphasized the importance of media literacy and critical thinking skills among audiences to discern reliable information from misleading or false content. Mobile journalists, in turn, must adopt strategies to combat the spread of misinformation while harnessing the reach of social media for news dissemination.

As we navigate this digital frontier, it is imperative for journalists, media organizations, and society at large to engage in ongoing discussions and research to ensure that mobile journalism continues to uphold the principles of accuracy, transparency, and ethical reporting. By leveraging the innovations highlighted in recent studies, mobile journalism can fulfil its potential as a powerful and democratizing force in the realm of news dissemination.

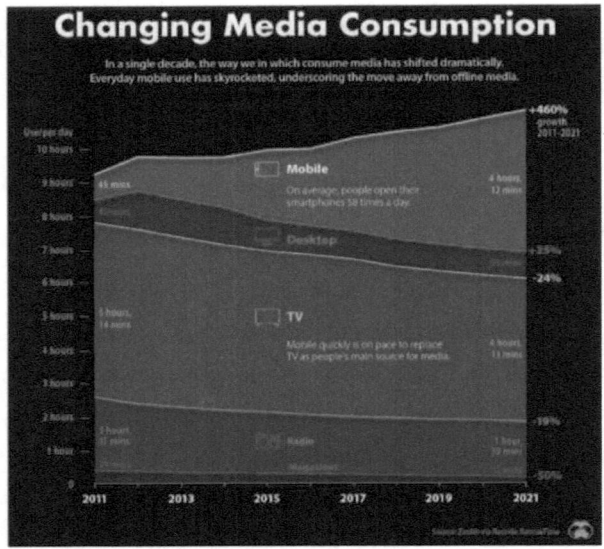

Fig. 8.2 Changing Media Consumption

Source: Zenith via Recode, RescueTime

Rise of User-Generated Content (UGC)

The prevalence of smartphones has empowered ordinary citizens to become active contributors to the news cycle. User generated content (UGC), often captured and shared through mobile devices, has become a valuable source of information for journalists and news organizations. A study conducted by the Reuters Institute for the Study of

Journalism found that 75% of news consumers encounter UGC on social media platforms, indicating its growing significance in the news ecosystem.

Mobile Journalism has led to an increased demand for shortform and visual content. Studies show that audiences, particularly younger demographics, prefer consuming news in bite-sized formats such as videos, infographics, and photo slideshows. The mobile-friendly nature of such content aligns with the on-the-go lifestyles of modern audiences, emphasizing the need for news organizations to adapt their storytelling techniques. This is one of the prime reasons for the adoption of Instagram stories and feeds over other social media, because of the urgency as well as distributing pint sized bites of information to a predominantly youth-oriented audience.

8.6 Mobile Journalism Internationally

In a large country like India, Indians themselves proudly proclaim, the world's biggest democracy with more than 400 television channels and over 9061 newspapers, according to the Registrar of Newspapers for India (RNI, 2017), mobile journalism is only to be expected. The Indian media are expanding in double digit growth rates and the active promotion of 5G connections and aggressive consumerism in the area of mobile phones has help promulgate the spread of citizen journalism even into the far corners of the country. Set up in 2002, a small group of amateur journalists called "Video Volunteers" began producing bite sized videos aimed at showcasing the problems of underprivileged people groups, the marginalised, with all their attendant problems. They made little progress initially, but now are much better known. Another mini group known as "India Unheard" also created waves by providing news services to mainstream channels and now have 249 correspondents with more than 6000 video reports. Yet another burgeoning alternative media channel is "MeriNews" which can be read as "MyNews". This was launched in 2006 (Allan, Sonwalkar, & Carter, 2007). Three years later another people group called WAVE (Women Aloud Videographing for Empowerment) was also started which enjoyed a fair amount of popularity at the local level. An organisation which started much later, but rapidly rising into prominence is CGNet Swara a news service who carry out filming and running video, through using smartphones, was started in 2010 and now sustains a thriving business, apart from gaining a reputation for credibility.

Some have received awards, some have not; but all of them have demonstrated visually and statistically, that if there is a channel that addresses genuine grievances immediately and that is committed to fight corruption and vouch for social justice, even if only at a local level, there is a measure of acceptance and viewership and very soon they can emerge as a major source of news feeds. Citizen reporting especially in the case of flagrant violation of human rights, have, on several occasions gained prominence, creating a profound impact on the mainstream news agenda.

Other Asian countries also have mixed response in the area of citizen journalism. In Vietnam, this form of journalism in the form of an active social media presence either on Twitter, or Youtube or Facebook (now Meta), gained a new boost. It is estimated that nearly 64% of the population were active social media users, spending over 2 hours on different platforms airing their views on multiple issues with a fair degree of boldness and resilience. This is remarkable in lieu of the fact that the ruling party is the Communist party who control all of the mainstream media. But insistent and regular use of social media has even forced to accept the presence of social media and recognise it as a forum for the intelligentsia in recent days.

In China, Xin (2010) investigating cases of citizen journalism in this communist ruled country found surprisingly that it played a fairly important role challenging the mainstream media on many fronts.

One incident of citizen journalism in China is well known. A local resident in Chongqing actively disobeyed an official order demanding that he move out of a property in which he was residing which was state owned. A young citizen journalist visited this "nail house" as it is locally known, and covered the story from a sympathetic angle highlighting how the residents, a young working-class couple were desperately fighting developers from a construction site. As a result of his persistent journalistic forays and daring blogging, public outrage was evoked, building up so much local pressure that ultimately the mainstream media also covered the event, and the couple were granted a respite from their struggles.

In other Asian countries also, citizen journalism is on the rise and rapidly gaining both acceptance as well as popularity. In Malaysia, a citizen forum called "Malaysiakini" trained numerous citizen journalists to produced news articles, videos and graphic images for their website. In this country at least, this vibrant challenge to mainstream journalism has shaken the "pillars of traditional journalism" and upset the applecart of many political parties, religious movements and conservative public forums. But in many places still there is active resistance, even hatred of this new and upcoming species of the Mobile journalist. On the surface seemingly taking this new form of journalism in their stride, yet we see in most of Southeast Asia, civic bodies and mainstream journalists continue their verbal and legal assault, threats, veiled or otherwise and insist on technological intervention and control, when they feel that matters are going out of hand and into the hands of an intensely aware and proactive public.

Traversing into other non-Asian countries, we find that even in Russia, the stronghold of communism and state-controlled media, citizen journalism does find occasional echoes of mainstream journalism; although a few outspoken voices did manage to rise above the stifling political blanket, throwing all caution to the winds, casting down the gauntlet of challenge. But these are occasional bubbles of resistance, rising to the surface rather than a concerted and consistent delivering of news that may border on the controversial, but is at least, within the realm of independent news coverage. The so-called "golden era" of Russian journalism lasted for only a short while between the eighties and the nineties after which,

> "The politicisation of the information system resumed (Koltsova, 2006, p. 37; Strovsky, 2011). During this period, "the role of media in the information system ceased to be independent". (Zassoursky, 2004, p. 29). Mass media became a means of manipulating, rather than enlightening or informing the audience".

Conclusion

The symbiotic relationship between technology and journalism has opened new avenues for storytelling, engagement, and accessibility. Mobile Journalism, with its roots firmly planted in the pockets of billions, has the potential to redefine the very essence of journalism in the digital age. However, as we navigate uncharted territories, it is imperative to address the challenges and ethical considerations that accompany this evolution, or rather revolution, ensuring that the principles of accuracy, fairness, and transparency which have always been the mainstay of news reporting, remain. It will be a while before the citizen journalist no matter how avid and how sincere, is accorded the same respect and credibility status as the mainstream journalist, but without a shadow of doubt, this new alternative form of media is on the rise. As already mentioned, this emergent trend has "shaken the traditional bastions of the established fourth estate" and in times to come, as new technological interventions continue to ascend and invade the market; as phones become exceedingly smarter, delivering data at higher data rates than is now prevailing, mobile journalism will slowly but inevitably, gain the upper hand!

References

Roberts, J. (2019). The erosion of ethics: From citizen journalism to social media. *Journal of Information, Communication and Ethics in Society*, *17*(4), 409–421.

https://doi.org/10.1108/JICES-01-2019-0014

Nah, S., & Chung, D. S. (2016). Communicative action and citizen journalism: A case study of OhmyNews in South Korea. *International Journal of Communication*, *10*, 21.

Naz, M., & Khan, M. (2023). Transformation in Journalism: Photojournalism in the Era of Augmented Reality.

Simons, G. (2016). The impact of social media and citizen journalism on mainstream Russian news. *Russian Journal of Communication*, *8*(1), 33–51.

https://doi.org/10.1080/19409419.2016.1140590

CHAPTER NINE

Artificial Intelligence and Machine Learning: The New Normal

9.1 Introduction

Artificial Intelligence (AI) and Machine Learning (ML) stand at the forefront of technological evolution, profoundly impacting the landscape of New Media. This chapter explores the recurrent relationship between AI/ML and New Media, delving into their applications, ethical implications, future trends, and the transformative potential they hold in shaping our digital experiences for real life.

9.2 Foundations of AI and ML

AI refers to the simulation of human intelligence processes by machines, encompassing learning, reasoning, and problem solving. ML, a subset of AI, involves systems learning from data, identifying patterns, and making decisions without the need for hard core programming. The integration of AI and ML has redefined the functionalities of New Media platforms, revolutionizing content creation, user interaction, and personalized experiences. From recommendation systems to content generation and predictive analytics, these technologies have surfaced as pivotal in reshaping digital content ecosystems. Along with AI and Machine Learning (ML) a technology which is growing fast and is a catalyst for the meteoric growth of AI, is blockchain. Blockchain was the technology behind the creation of NFTs, which has taken the financial as well as creative media/entertainment worlds by storm. These non-fungible tokens, along with blockchain form the nucleus of what is now known as the 'Metaverse' and which has grown from a remote science fiction ephemeral concept into a tangible reality.

Today there is no field in which we do not encounter AI. Whether it is creating a visiting card or a poster on "Canva", modifying an edit in "Veed.io" or even commanding (through voice control), the windows of souped-up cars to roll down or roll up, AI has made its insidious presence felt everywhere. Most netizens welcome AI as it has removed the drudgery of many tasks and made easier hitherto esoteric crafts and skills like 3D motion and graphics and complex photography, many express unmitigated concern about how AI will affect the professional industry especially the graphics and animation industry as software which took years to learn and master earlier, now deliver stunning results - thanks to complex algorithms, which merge, collate and synthesis many keywords and key concepts to come up with complex graphics with sometimes unimaginable visual effects.

Perhaps these eager "new kids on the block" armed with a sophisticated repertoire of skills and techniques, ready to ply them effectively to the most daunting animation challenge, need to pay attention to Elon Musk's statement. Musk long ago, anticipating the tremendous impact that AI would play in our personal and professional lives, reiterated the old adage, which surfaced sometime in the 1940s, that "if you can't beat 'em', join 'em".

Editing, animation and visual effects crafts which took many years to master and many months to execute have now moved from the domain of the expert into the domain of the novice or at least the tech savvy young enthusiast. But in order to understand the real power of AI and how it is going to influence the generations to come, we first need to delve a little bit into the history of it, early probings and how what originally fell into the realm of science fiction has now been actualized into a tangible reality!

We first had a little peek into how AI might dominate the life of a human being in Stanley Kubrick's magnum Opus "2001: A Space Odyssey". The year 2001 has now long gone, but when the script was first written and the story first filmed and edited between 1967-68. In the film, "HAL" a supercomputer controls the life of a lone astronaut in outer space, including making subtle suggestions like what he should wear and what he should eat. The film was well ahead of its time as it portrayed the state of loneliness which encompasses many of us who are overwhelmed by technology; and also predicted the coming of super computers that would begin, like Skynet in the famous "Terminator' series encapsulated by visionary filmmaker James Cameron, that would ultimately control every aspect of our lives!

But that was in the past where vague and abstract suggestions were put forward about the impending doom that AI would ultimately wreak upon humanity. But AI is not all negative.

Although it does, to some extent, take the control out of our hands and place them in the armatures of a robot or automaton, this can be a tremendous boon to humanity. AI now finds applications everywhere - from booking a Uber cab to giving verbal instructions to a an advanced car model, to a housewife using an automated robot to vacuum clean her house; AI has made inroads into all areas of human endeavour and activity. To those in the medical diagnostics and therapeutic industries, it can indeed be a life saver and can greatly cut costs and step up production in the industrial sector, thereby liberating the factory worker from many tasks of drudgery, and also by streamlining production processes and pipelines, can render them highly efficient, and thereby reduce the cost of a product. This benefit can be reaped by the consumer, who rather than fearing how AI might take away his job, be grateful for the added advantage he is gaining through implementation of this new technology.

9.3 Early Origins of Artificial Intelligence

AI while developed as a concept and application only recently, had its origins as far back as the nineteenth century when scientists like Allen Newell, Simon and George Boole founded the first artificial intelligence laboratory way back in the years between 1815 and 1864.

But the real brains behind AI, or who can easily be called as the father of AI, was Alan Turing. Turing wrote a paper in 1936 on "computable numbers". This paper contained the essential elements of what would later constitute a "Computer", but it was his paper entitled "Computing Machinery and Intelligence" written years later that would become the basis for development of a real artificial intelligence system. Turing was also the person responsible for the creation of the famous "Turing test" which was a game style approach to determine if a computer could outwit a human being, and thereby proving to the world that it was an "intelligent device". Since then AI has been passing through many "hoops" and "loops". But like in every other field, progress in this field too has been steady and inexorable. In 2018, Google's master mind, Sundar Pichai announced to the world at large, that Google Assistant, an AI application that responds to voice input was truly intelligent. He asked the assistant on a mobile phone to fix up an appointment with a local hairdresser, an instruction with which the device politely complied with, without hesitation or errors. Although many were very impressed with this massive leap of technology, it was not without its critics, as some expressed their disapproval by saying that the communication was unilateral and not bidirectional, as human communication usually is. Another vociferous critic of new technologies is John Searle, who in 1980 wrote a paper called "Minds, Brains and Programs" where he experimentally set up a "Chinese Room Argument" to bring to public knowledge, all possible defects in an artificial intelligence device or instrument.

Another wry critic of AI systems, even AI as a concept, was Hubert Dreyfus, author of the book "What Computers Still Can't do: A Critique of Artificial Reason".

He was extremely sceptical of the power of AI and felt that it would never at any stage be comparable to the latent power of the human brain and intellect.

Along with Turin another scientist who contributed greatly to the further development of AI technology was McCarthy, who is credited with having developed the LISP programming language which is used with AI projects because of how easily it can work with nonnumerical data. McCarthy was a prolific inventor and scientist who in addition to developing LISP also formulated the concept of time sharing of computers. He along with another pioneer, also co-founded MIT's artificial intelligence laboratory. McCarthy shares his inventing genius with another pioneer Rosenblatt, who developed so many concepts on the inner workings of neural networking that the New York Times extolled Rosenblatt's concept of the "perceptron" as being a computer that could "walk, talk, see, write and even be conscious of its own existence". Obviously, such accolades were more a stretch of the imagination and a result of eulogizing the scientific genius of Rosenblatt, but this led to greatly increased interest in the promotion of AI and some years later in the 1950s, Minsky developed a very crude neural network machine using tubes and spare parts. Although Minsky had spent considerable time and effort on the development of this crude predecessor of the current sophisticated AI systems, Minsky very quickly realised that this would not stand the test of time and decided to spend his creative energies in other directions.

If the 40s and the 50s were the supposedly "boom" period for the development of AI systems, during the 1970s, enthusiasm for this non-human form of intelligence began to die down and AI development entered what would be known as the "AI winter". Very soon scientists and entrepreneurs realised that the "LISP" language which was the primary programming language for AI systems had many drawbacks and loopholes and interest shifted to FORTRAN, that seemed much more robust in its programmability. There was considerable global economic instability also in the 70s with the middle east oil crisis, steadily mounting inflation and regressive growth. Funds for scientific innovation and progress were slow in forthcoming and finances were diverted into other more lucrative sectors. But despite the slowdown in the progress achieved in AI systems thus far, there were still innovations happening in the background.

Backpropagation was a feature for assigning weights to neural networks, and this was supplemented by work done on recurrent neural networks, a system or protocol which allowed for connections to move through input and output layers. AI naturally paved the way for what is now known as expert systems, an early example of which is XCON developed by John McDermott at Carnegie Mellon University. From the time it was first launched in 1980, it turned out to be a big time and cost saver, and XCON turned out to be such a huge success that it triggered the boom in expert systems, and investments for this hitherto stagnant industry began to resurface as the AI industry was now once again poised for a new comeback.

Expert systems were what helped IBM to build its "deep blue" computer that defeated grandmaster Gary

Kasparov in a historic and long stretched chess match, way back in 1966. Many others made substantial contributions to the development of AI into a fully workable and configurable system. Some names that stand out in this field who have not already been mentioned are Geoffrey Hinton, who made several contributions, inspired by the initial groundwork of Rosenblatt and another pathbreaking scientist was Fei-Li, a scientist with a PhD in Electrical Engineering from Caltech, who with the help of 'Mechanical Turk', an online resource that relied on crowd funding, created 'ImageNet' which culled 3.2 million images over 5,200 categories. If one talks of Big Data, that was an early example of humungous 'Big Data'!

9.4 The importance of Big Data

As expert systems, computers and AI all deal with data, it is worth spending some time here explaining the significance of data. There are essentially four ways to organise data. But in terms of actual data, there are primarily two types of data recognised by expert systems and AI. These are:

(a) Structured Data

(b) Unstructured Data

Structured data, generally stored in the form of a relational database can include financial information, addresses, point of sale data or even phone numbers.

But for the most part, the data base in the computer would consist of unstructured data. Some examples of unstructured data would be:

(a) Images

(b) Audio files

(c) Video files

(d) text files and

(e) Satellite images

Apart from these two intrinsic forms of data, there is also a huge category of data known as 'Hybrid Data'. Author Akin Ünver calls hybrid data as that which,

> "refers to the multi-purpose nature of human footprint online; namely, how people's 'like's, retweets and check-in decisions can be harvested to be cross-fed into each other to generate a multidimensional snapshot of micro and macro-level determinants of social behavior".[1]

Hybrid data comes between the two types of data mentioned earlier i.e structured and unstructured and introduces a third category and that is semi-structured data. Some examples of semistructured data include XML (Extensible Markup Language) and JSON (Javascript Object Notation) which is a method of transferring information through the web. But all artificial systems, regardless of the magnitude of their operations crunch volumes and volumes of numbers - hence the term Big Data. There is as such no definition of Big Data, but Gartner analyst Doug Laney attributed three qualities to big data and that is (i) Volume (ii) Variety and (iii) Velocity.

> "Every second, Google processes over 40,000 searches or 3.5 billion a day. On a minute-by-minute basis, Snapchat users share 527,760 photos, and YouTube users watch more than 4.1 million videos. Then there are the old-fashioned systems, like emails, that continue to see significant growth".[2]

Not only is the volume of data handled voluminous, but it costs organisations and firms a huge amount of dollar spends also. According to IDC, Big Data and Analytic solutions is forecasted to go from $166 billion in 2018 to $260 billion by 2022. (Ibid)

This naturally begets the question, if organisations are spending such large amounts of money on this unique form of data, and it is causing such a massive drain on the exchequer, then is it worth it? To answer the question, we need to first examine how much data is presently available, how much more is needed and what can actually be done with the gargantuan databases that exist in servers all around the world. Primary use of big data is in business applications although it does find a place in the entertainment industry as well. Generally speaking, AI in business is used to make realistic projections, detect faults in production and financial pipelines and help the management take business decisions that will yield long term benefits and ROIs.

Analytics can be used to determine root causes of failure of particular business strategies adopted in the past, detect fraudulent behavior and greatly improve the efficacy of preconceived marketing strategies. All this translates to Megabucks and hence the imminent need for Big Data!

But big data is not just confined to the squeaky-clean air-conditioned corridors of business houses alone. They also find a very useful place in academic institutions. Apart from being a very current and useful field of study for students, AI is also useful for educators, by providing with them with new tools to help identify weak and at-risk students, develop and refine their curriculum, and streamline scheduling of various events that are the hallmark of any good academic institution. It can greatly assist in provide self-paced coaching to weaker students and help them with internships and job placements as and when the need arises.

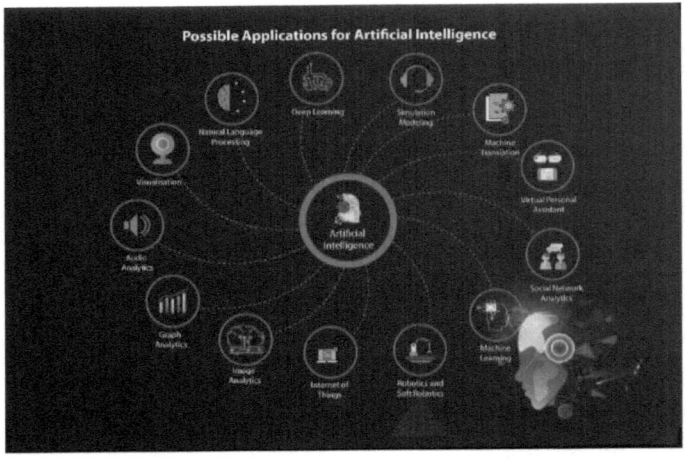

Fig 9.1: Possible Applications of Artificial Intelligence

9.5 Applications of AI

Many large companies and multinationals are now using AI to drive sales and marketing. The MNC giant, MacDonald began to use a AI package known as dynamic yield, the technology of which was used to more or less reinvent its "Drive Thru" facility, which accounts for a major portion of the sales inventory of McDonald. The AI technology analyses statistics and data gathered about the weather, time of day, traffic conditions etc., and based on this data, digital menus are dynamically adjusted. This was seen to be very instrumental in affecting sales pick up at peak seasons. McDonald's are now using AI regularly for their in-store kiosks and signage as well. AI has found vast and diverse applications in the medical field. Not just in diagnostics and imaging but in therapeutic care as well

Scholars Basu, Sinha and Ong have done extensive research in applications of AI in medical science and medical research and state that,

> "Applications of AI in the field of medical sciences include matching patient symptoms to appropriate physician, patient diagnosis, patient prognosis, drug discovery, bot assistant that can translate languages, transcribe notes, and organize images and files". [3]

Thus, for example in dermatology, AI has been used to develop classification models in the diagnosis of skin cancer, skin lesions and psoriasis. In the area of diabetes and diabetic care, researchers at Google trained a DCNN using "28,175 retinal fundus images to classify images as diabetic retinopathy and macular oedema for adults with diabetes" In the area of drug discovery, Verge Genomics used machine learning algorithms to identify drugs that could be used to fend off neurological diseases like Parkinson's disease and amyotrophic lateral sclerosis (ALS) effectively. Apart from direct interventions such as these, AI systems are also being used indirectly in assisting in many administrative processes like scheduling appointments, tracing which physicians are on call duty in large hospitals and listing all the available drugs and clinical tools through customisable medical apps, thereby contributing to the general efficiency and smooth running of the hospital administration and other non-medical departments in large clinics or hospitals.

While definitely medical imaging diagnostics and treatment is a huge area of applications of AI, the entertainment industry is not lagging far behind in the advanced application of AI in fields where it is really needed. The most obvious example is in the field of gaming and animation; the development of game assets, advanced 3D animations software. Even a relatively simple graphic package like Adobe Photoshop is now using advanced AI technology for the automatic generation of fantasy images. Enter the Virtual Reality dimension and Augmented Reality. These advanced simulation engines and computing intensive software simply cannot be functional unless driven by AI simulation and rendering technologies.

Gaming has gone a long way from the simple PacMan and Prince of Persia of yore, and is now yoked to AI tools and technologies which seamlessly synchromesh together to create a truly unique, captivating immersive experience that is truly mind bending!

AI has taken giant strides in the music industry as well. Typical user data like type of music preference, selected compositions, listening history and playlist preferences. All these are analysed by music recommendation system, which then create a unique profile of the listener and then draw from the user profile to proffer helpful suggestions that hopefully will greatly enhance the listening experience.

If one enters the realm of post-production, here also, AI can certainly be put to useful and professional use, as audio mastering necessarily implies use of many tools, software and custom presets to create cutting edge and error free music. Much of tedious repetitive cyclical work is now taken care of AI assisted audio mastering to create a sound envelope or music that is truly enthralling and a complete sensory experience.

Another area using AI with which all can identify with is "Netflix". Netflix is arguably one of the largest OTT platform in the world with millions of movies being streamed online to the cosy comfort of your homes. And it uses smart AI technology, based on viewing habits and historical preferences to make intelligent predictive guesses as to what movie or serial you would want to watch next. Some welcome this feature; many find it irritating and presumptuous. But the fact is that the technology is here to stay and whether the user likes it or not, AI will continue to grow and expand in the entertainment industry in all sectors - be it Radio, Television, Films, Videos or Podcasts.

Today, the movie industry relies heavily on AI technologies to brainstorm, write skeleton scripts and storyboards, and of course, no post-production could be regarded as complete, or even professional, without the use of AI tools integrated seamlessly into the software.

9.6 Machine Learning

This is the new mantra that is plying the AI and related industries market presently. Computer critics in the seventies and eighties kept bemoaning the fact that while computers were undoubtedly smart (even in that infantile era), they would never match up to human standards as smart as they were, they were not "smart" enough to learn and adapt the way that humans could. But presently it appears that current massive leaps in Machine Learning technologies and systems, is turning that old criticism on its head. We have all witnessed how silently computers that are undergoing errors or gaps in handshaking are now beginning to mend and repair themselves, and these self-diagnostics and auto heal mechanisms have been made possible through machine learning.

The history of Machine Learning (ML) can be traced back to pioneering attempts at MIT and Bell Telephone Laboratories by Arthur Samuel. He was the man behind the building of the 701, IBM's first commercial computer and also developed the computer checkers game which can today be regarded as the first prototype of a machine learning system. We have already seen how Alan Turing took the first baby steps towards introducing first generation computers to the waiting world. Tentative technological steps were then later taken by John McCarthy, Allan Newell and Herbert Simon from Carnegie-Mellon University. The next milestone came in the form of "The Perceptron" devised by a technological genius, Rosenblatt, who was not a scientist, but rather a psychologist by profession. The idea behind the "Perceptron" is the same idea that propels machine learning - and that is that computers, can, and do learn from past mistakes.

The methods that any machine learning system follow, can be classified into four major parts, or processes,

(i) Supervised Learning

(ii) Unsupervised Learning

(iii) Semi-supervised learning and finally

(iv) Reinforced Learning

Supervised learning is where datasets that are accurately labelled are used to "train" or program algorithms to classify data and predict outcomes accurately by making comparisons with previous outcomes. A model exists in the computer, and as data is inputted, associated weights are adjusted until a "best fit" of the model has been appropriated. This is an essential part of a cross-validation process which ensures both accuracy and predictability of systems using that data. This finds many real-world examples of perhaps which an example which recurs daily is the separation of spam filter from genuine messages in a mailbox.

The other form of learning is when some training labels are missing. These can range from weakly supervised learning methods to weakly supervised learning methods. The extent to which a particular method is semi-supervised depends on how the labels are created. Where they are "noisy" or "imprecise", the less effective the learning model is.

The final category of machine learning is unsupervised learning where the only information that is being uploaded is inputs. This depends a lot on the optimism of the developers who believe, truly or falsely that they have programmed the machine to such an extent that it can run flawlessly and is intelligent enough to be "intuitive" and "inventive" as well as auto correct itself. Naturally, this implies creations of programs and algorithms that are extremely robust and adaptive, which may not always be the case.

The reinforcement learning method is a method that is concerned with how software agents should take action in certain environments to maximize some notion of cumulative reward. Reinforcement learning is often used in game theory, operations research, control theory, information theory, multi-agent systems, stimulation-based optimization, statistics, swarm intelligence, and genetic algorithms.

Reinforced learning finds applications in numerous fields like swarm intelligence, game theory and in stimulation-based optimization. A common example of reinforced learning is where a computer is pitted against a human being (for example the famous chess match of Garry Kasparov versus the "Deep Blue" intelligent computer). Machines in this kind of learning environment use sophisticated algorithms to make moves that are not easily predictable and often difficult to detect.

ML finds more applications in field that one would have though possible.

The table below encapsulates some of the numerous practical applications of ML.

S.NO	MACHINE LEARNING APPLICATION
1	Technology Industry
2	Adaptive websites
3	Affective computing
4	Computer networks
5	Computer vision
6	Data quality
7	General game playing
8	Information retrieval
9	Internet fraud detection
10	Machine learning control
11	Machine perception
12	Machine translation
13	Optimization
14	Recommend systems
15	Robot locomotion

16	Search engines
17	Sequence Mining
18	Software engineering
19	Speech recognition
20	Syntax pattern recognition
21	Telecommunication
22	Theorem proving
23	Time series forecasting
24	Agricultural Industry
25	Medical Industry
26	Anatomy
27	Bioinformatics
28	Brain-machine interfaces
29	Cheminformatics
30	DNA sequence classification
31	Medical diagnosis
32	Structural health monitoring
33	Financial Industry
34	Banking
35	Credit-card fraud detection
36	Economics
37	Financial market analysis
38	Insurance
39	Marketing
40	Online advertising
41	Human Behaviour Industry
42	Handwriting recognition
43	Linguistics
44	Natural language processing
45	Natural language understanding
46	Sentiment analysis
47	User behaviour analytics

Table 9.1: Uses of Machine Learning

Conclusion

The next step would for intelligent computers to take would be perhaps, where they have "emotions", 'feel' the need for affirmation, and maybe even who knows, develop an "ego" that they are in reality, truly more intelligent than the beings who created them. When compared to humans, often an observation is made that human beings have a sense of self-awareness. That is being able to ask, and often also self-answer, ontological questions such as what is the meaning and purpose of life, where do I come from, where am I headed etc. All religions, and even many scientists too believe that humans have a "soul" whose existence is impossible to prove, but whose subtle innate presence leaves an indelible mark on our lives. Perhaps the next generation of "super intelligent" computers would have feelings, emotions, perhaps even worry, if they are really up to the mark. But that is more a matter of conjecture and perhaps best left to the authors of science fiction than a matter of discussion in a book of this nature. But one conclusion is inescapable. And that is that both AI and ML are here to stay. They are going to be constantly improved, enhanced and updated - and will make increasing inroads into our daily existence and activities. It is the "smart" Netizen who will accept, challenge or reject this imminent reality. The "intelligent" choice is up to him or her!

References

Taulli, T. (2019). *Artificial Intelligence Basics: A Non-Technical Introduction*. Apress. https://doi.org/10.1007/978-1-4842-5028-0

[2] Ünver, H. A. (2024). *Artificial Intelligence, Authoritarianism and the Future of Political Systems*.

[3] Taulli, T. (2019). *Artificial Intelligence Basics: A Non-Technical Introduction*. Apress. https://doi.org/10.1007/978-1-4842-5028-0

[4] Basu, K., Sinha, R., Ong, A., & Basu, T. (2020). Artificial intelligence: How is it changing medical sciences and its future?. *Indian journal of dermatology*, 65(5), 365-370.

CHAPTER TEN

Burgeoning of the Metaverse: VR and AR parallel worlds

10.1 Introduction

In recent years one word which is surfacing with increasing regularity, making waves especially amongst the tech savvy youths, is the term "Metaverse". TV serials, movies, books and web series all seem to be overflowing with copies references to the "Metaverse". A dystopian universe which parallels our present world and where the real and the unreal mesh seamlessly with each other, where the most outlandish fantastical dreams can be realised and enjoyed in a metaphysical world. A world which has its own currency, its own economy, its own physical and natural laws, and where secrecy is literally, 'virtually' non-existent. Welcome to the Metaverse, a fluctuating pulsating continually reorganising universe where all known and recognised and systems are in a constant state of flux and reorganisation.

The term "Metaverse" was invented by writer Neal Stephenson in his novel "Snow Crash" published in 1992. In this Universe, displaying modernized shades of Fritz Lang's "Metropolis", humans masquerading as Avatars interact with intelligent agents in a world portrayed as a Metropolis, developed along a neon-lit hundred metre wide boulevard with the single uncreative name of "Street". The street traverses the circumference of a huge planet that has been visited by 120 million users. Out of this large number, at any one given time, only 15 million occupy it.

Presently, the "Metaverse" is simply a concept, and words are just being thrown around without understanding the full complexities of the Metaverse or its exacting demands on hardware and software. Movies like James Cameron's "Avatar" and "Dr Strange: Into the Multiverse Madness" have all helped whip up excitement over this new hi-tech toy that threatens to dominate the future of entertainment and gaming, but can this overhyped so-called synthetic "Metaverse" really replace the present Universe? Will human civilisation allow themselves to be so immersed into technology and virtual culture that they can no longer distinguish virtual from the real? This is a real existential dilemma that needs to be resolved before one delves into the technicalities that surround it.

This chapter looks at some of the myths surrounding the Metaverse, opportunities, implications and ramifications. And the path the Metaverse will traverse in the near future.

10.2 History of the Metaverse

On October 28th, 2021, the CEO of the widely used Facebook which had become a household name in all active Internet circles, announced that it would now no longer continue with that name. It was christened as "Meta" an indication of the increasing role that this word would play in all spheres of human endeavour and technical structures.

The term "Metaverse" itself is an amalgamation of two words

"Meta" and "Universe". The word "Meta" itself means "Transcending" and was first coined by Neal Stephenson in his pioneering novel "Snowcrash".

While "Snowcrash" was not really a best seller in the pure sense of the word, it did introduce both the word, and the concept, and the moniker stuck.

Many people envisage the Metaverse as the next iteration of the Internet. A universe which supports immersive interactive and very realistic digital simulation and representations of the real world. Like the web, the Metaverse is not a single isolated place, but exists very much like how the brain is organised in that some facts are stored in not one location, but in multiple locations. And there is a strong tendency for many to associate the Metaverse with Gaming, but in reality, the Metaverse is much more than that, with gaming being only one of its' best-known components.

All avid readers of science fiction would have read the books the legendary science fiction writer, Arthur C. Clarke who created a law, which he called the "Third" law which states that "any sufficiently advanced technology is indistinguishable from magic."

Other writers, perhaps having vaguely conceived of the Metaverse, have attributed other nicknames to it. Designer and writer Charlie Maggie, came up in 1993 with, in true resonance of Alan Toffler's evolutionary "waves" or "ages" as he termed it - the "Imagination Age". In this, Magee predicted that this will be an era where most of the routine manual tasks would be replaced by robots; and automation would be the driving force of this age, where man would be co-dependent with machines and robots for day-to-day functioning technology.

But the origins of the Metaverse trace back to much earlier than Arthur C. Clarke's path breaking novel or Charles Maggie's the "Imagination Age". It appears that the Metaverse as a realisable concept was driven by multiple factors such as ideology, innovations in technology, eCommerce and of course, the unfathomable imagination of the human mind.

It is a well-known fact that many works of fiction, especially science fiction, are what inspires innovators and scientists to put theoretical concepts to the test in the lab, and so it was that books such as Gibsons'

"Neuromancer" and the movie "Torn" in 1982, stirred the imagination of many. This led to several early experiments, dabbling in what is known today as 'Virtual Reality'. The term itself was first coined by the French poet and playwright Antonin Artaud in his collection of essays entitled "The Theatre and its Double". This was promptly followed by the 'Sensorama', the first prototype of not 3D, but 4D simulation as fans and odours were used to augment the sense of realism of a 3D movie of a motorbike travelling through New York City. Such novel innovations may seem tacky to todays' millennial generation looking at the world through Apple Vision Pro VR headsets, but at the time of its creation, machines like the 'Sensorama' spawned a vigorous interest in 3D, headsets and similar gadgets so that the entertainment experience could be taken to the next level.

Movies such as "Ready Player One" have added to the "meta" hype in more ways than one, lending an air of mysticism and inexplicability to an already convoluted parallel universe.

"The Matrix", a pioneering, mind bending science fiction movie, which is now embedded as a legend in the annals of the science fiction genre of movies, created not just ripples, but huge breakers, of what a future where matter could be moulded according to one's will, might hold. "Tron" in 1982, set the cinematic stage for the 'Metaverse', followed by movies such as the "Thirteenth Floor" in 1999, directed by Josef Rusnak and "Ready Player One" in 2018, directed by the legendary science fiction and action/thriller movie filmmaker, Steven Spielberg.

The screenplay was written by Zak Penn and Cline and portrays a future set in 2045, from which we are not very far now, where nearly all of humanity take recourse to a virtual reality simulation nicknamed the "Oasis" to escape all the mundane problems of human existence. In true Spielbergian tradition, the film was cinematically excellent, the scenes breathtaking in their intensity and visualisation and it triggered the imagination of countless young and not so young minds, that such a futuristic concept may not be so phantasmagorical after all, and could one very well one day turn from virtual into a concrete reality. But it was the development of technology - of 3D software, of gaming in 3D and the manufacture of increasingly sophisticated headsets which enabled one to "see" and configure the "Meta" landscape so to speak. This will be examined in greater depth, in the sections that follow.

10. 3 Characteristics of the Metaverse

Privacy of all habits will be a thing of the past in the Metaverse. At present Websites, thanks to Google Analytics, collect all the data about your surfing habits, websites visited number of likes, clicks on certain buttons etc. And based on this personalised browsing history, collected through the cookies that become activated every time you click on the button "Accept all cookies", your likes, dislikes, preferences, shopping habits; all habits that can lend themselves to possible commercial gains are logged and recorded and then possible websites that can offer related products are pasted alongside your current website by way of polite suggestion. This recent phenomenon which has acquired the name of "dataveillance", is essentially observation of all online actions, recording of them, and then sophisticated algorithms track one's buying habits, even separating casual surfing from serious buying, and ads related to choices made or see, pop up. In the case of Disney's Magic Kingdom for example, the Megacorporation has moved beyond video cameras and plainclothesmen following a tourist to the digital realm. Now Disney apps record most of your actions to know exactly what you are doing in a theme park, and if you happen to be wearing a MyMagic+ wristband, then Disney can even come to know where you stopped for a snack, or if you are in a queue to purchase tickets, or simply relaxing at one of the various resorts and enjoying the view.[1]

In a book on the Metaverse, Andrew Clemens narrates a story of a woman who is hungry and while passing a pastry shop, stops to gaze at some cakes and pastries there. Her movements which are recorded in the Metaverse, immediately deduce that she is hungry and so the next time she proceeds to surf any website she is deluged with a flood of food ads. We see this happening all the time, and this is one of the technical offshoots of the Metaverse and along with its numerous beneficial gains one of the caveats also. In order for the Metaverse to be implementable and truly beneficial, it is necessary that certain parameters be taken care of.[2]

First and foremost, it should be,

(1) **Inclusive**. It should not be limited to a few techno geeks and those with a penchant for gaming. For the Metaverse to gain truly universal acceptance, it needs to be easy to understand, follow and comprehend. Tools and utilities available on the Metaverse should be facile and easily transferable.

It's also important that the Metaverse be **Innovative**. New concepts like Cryptocurrency, Blockchain technology and NFTs are already concepts that are completely new and innovative. But these are becoming common parlance and acceptable in everyday conversation because of the slow but inexorable inroads that the Metaverse is making into each of our lives.

Privacy is another matter of concern. Any data shared over the Internet, while it may be made available to other users, the final copyright of usage remains with the originator of the data, and it is imperative that this data is not corrupted, misappropriated or analysed or reused without the explicit consent of the owner.

Although Intellectual Property Rights do exist in the Metaverse, it operates on a different plane in Cyberspace than it does in the real world.

Another factor that is often neglected is **Fair Use**. Value creation and Asset creation is an integral part of the Metaverse and it is essential that any fees or tariffs charged, should be reasonable and fair. Players in the Metaverse who make the maximum contribution should simultaneously also receive the maximum rewards, which usually takes place not in the medium of currency as we understand it, but in Cryptocurrencies, the accepted financial transactional medium of this new parallel world.

Yet another criterion for operating in the Metaverse is **Transparency**. Since there are no physical contracts here with hidden or discretely disguised clauses, it is important that all transactions take place in the Metaverse with complete transparency and all parties mutually engaged in, are fully aware of the stakes involved regardless of whether they are high or low.

Another critical characteristic of the Metaverse would be a **Decentralised Environment.**

> "...Decentralization in the context of the metaverse is all about proving ownership of (digital) assets and having full control over your identity, reputation, and data (self- sovereignty)".

What do we mean by decentralisation? Essentially it comes down to proving your ownership of digital assets. It can also mean that you have both full access as well as control over your data, identity and your image or reputation. Many feel that decentralisation is all about using blockchain technology to decentralise data storage or cut down on computing resources or about using the minimum bandwidth needed. But in reality, block chain is much more of a game changer and involves much more development of the application technology before we can start using it effectively to power the Metaverse.

This feature of the Metaverse is very critical to it because it helps the user to control censorship and also enables the end user to place their cryptographic trust in a vague and trust less environment. It also means that the onus of ownership has now shifted from Big Tech companies to the community and in that sense power that was concentrated in the hands of a chosen elitist few is now decentralised and made available to the masses. It is generally regarded that Ethereum was the first decentralised world that was fully owned by users.

Right now, the Metaverse is still in its infancy, so there are many views debates and discussions around it, most of which are pure speculation and not grounded in scientific fact. Says Laurence Lannom, vice president at the Corporation for National Research Initiatives,

"The metaverse will, at its core, be a collection of new and extended technologies. It is easy to imagine that both the best and the worst aspects of our online lives will be extended by being able to tap into a more-complete immersive experience, by being inside a digital space instead of looking at one from the outside. At the good end of the continuum are things like the ability of people to interact with others as though they were all in the same physical space without having spent hours burning dinosaur bones to get there; practicing difficult physical tasks (e.g., surgery) on virtual entities; and elevated educational and research opportunities of all kinds as we learn to leverage the built in advantages of the new environments.[3]

The boom in social media sites and the amount of time spent on them has given a huge fillip to the Metaverse, so much so that Facebook even changed its name to Meta. Many people, especially young adults are so enraptured by this alternative existence that they live "virtual" lives on these sites and so the Metaverse, at least in its 2D "Avatar" has already come into existence and is reshaping our lives.

Apart from social media sites, it has generally been observed that young people spend a large portion of their time in gaming. This serves not only as a stress buster but also sharpens their visual acuity so that they can work faster on the computer, discern complex situations more easily and also helps them in formulating attack strategies. Many of which of them will actually prove useful to them should they decide to opt for a career in the military or in the corporate sector

10.4 Gaming and the Metaverse

Despite being at the locus of numerous contestable debates, much confusion exists about the Metaverse and the scope of gaming within it, as many do not have a clear definition about it. Movies such as Ready Player One and others have portrayed the Metaverse as a single complex, yet unitarian entity that exists in virtual space. But in reality, the Metaverse, both ontologically as well as technically, exists in multiple dimensions, a point graphically illustrated in the block buster movie, "Dr Strange in the Multiverse of Madness". Spence (2008) has defined a more succinct and more precise definition of the Metaverse which he describes as

> " ... persistent, synthetic, three dimensional, non-game centric space"; making a distinction between games and social spaces. No such distinction is made here, because (social) play can be considered part of gaming "(Nevelsteen, K. J. L. (2018).[4]

In no other facet of the Metaverse has there been so much growth or speculation about growth than in the gaming sector. In fact, the two terms are almost interchangeably used and many have come to identify the Metaverse with gaming, when truth be told, they are actually two separate but co-dependent entities. In the Metaverse, it is alarmingly facile for players to lock virtual horns across the globe in a mind-bending, pulse racing game of Roblox or Minecraft. It is this interoperability on such a gargantuan scale that has led to a phenomenal growth of a technology dominated gaming industry that has spawned the growth of Virtual Reality (VR) and Augmented Reality (AR) immersive environments.

The graph below shows the global Augmented and Virtual Reality Gaming Market between 2021 and 2025 and the massive outlays and growth that has taken place in the last few years.

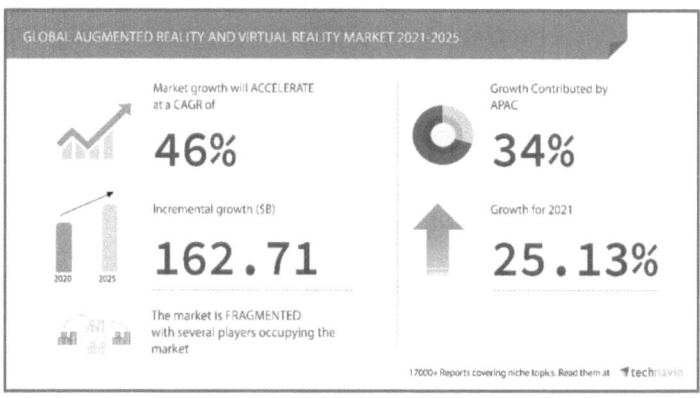

Fig 10.1: Global Augmented Reality and Virtual Reality Market
2021-2025
Source: technavio.com

The prime mover behind such rapid and unprecedented growth rates is the commerce and big stakes involved. The BigTech companies are looking at the big bucks and when it comes to gaming, the buck stops there. A report on the gaming industry on the web states that,

> "The global gaming market size was valued at USD 249.55 billion in 2022 and is anticipated to grow from USD 281.77 billion in 2023 to USD 665.77 billion by 2030, exhibiting a CAGR of 13.1% during the forecast period (2023-2030)".[5]

Simply because of Augmented and Virtual Reality alone, GDP globally has risen from 1.5 trillion in 2030 to an estimated $ 476.4 billion in 2025. In India alone, the gaming industry encompasses 500 million potential gamers and a net worth of $1 billion. However, compared to western countries, revenue gained through the Metaverse and investment in Meta accessories such as consoles and headsets is relatively less, partly due to the economic status of India, which is still to move into the welfare state bracket and partly due to the general mindset of the Indian public which sees expenditure on this market segment as frivolous and wasteful, when are there other more pressing concerns at hand. But notwithstanding, globally the meta verse and gaming operate on Mega dollars and it is seen by market analysts as one of the most profitable ventures in the present century.

Not only are transactions, investments and revenue garnered on a mammoth scale, but partly the reason for this high and continuous transactions is because of the complete turnaround in the nature of transactions in the Internet. Or to put it another way, the main medium of currency in the Metaverse is Cryptocurrency of which Non-Fungible Tokens or NFTs for short, play a significant role.

10.5 Non-Fungible Tokens (NFTs)

Sudden and palpable interest in Non-fungible Tokens which we will hitherto refer to as NFTs grew substantially after the third annual "NFT.NYC" which took place in November 2021 in Midtown Manhattan. This was attended by thousands who flocked to discover this new and revolutionary form of cryptocurrency. It was a mixed lot at the conference comprising of presenters, participants and exhibitors too. The conference features many panel discussions as well as heated debates on the validity of this new currency, its applications and most important, the measure of security and protection against cyber theft guaranteed by a currency that had not been tested on a large scale. NFTs arose because of the intrinsic nature of digitalisation. Once all material, be it for entertainment or for education is placed in the digital domain, it is relatively easy to replicate, duplicate and replace assets. This has acutely challenged traditional notions and rules of copyright and intellectual property protection. This cyber or crypto decentralised environment in which digital assets can be traded/exchanged purchased or sold with relative ease has given birth to NFTs as the *'de facto'* currency standard of the Metaverse.

Unlike other currencies, they just cannot be exchanged at face value. At present, NFTs have not only captured our imagination, it has also captured trading in the world of digital art and there is the story of a twelve-year-old who earned approximately $400,000 through selling some NFT art in the summertime. Virtual artwork has been sold for a staggering US $69.3 million. Large International food chains such as McDonald's and Burger King have begun to 'capitalise' on the growing popularity of NFTs and are now in the process of acquiring digital "collectibles".

Although NFTs have made "breaking news" in the world of digital arts and assets, its real value lies in,

> "providing unambiguous, decentralized ownership of non-physical goods such as memes, music, online property, gaming equipment — and, one day, even identity itself – by enabling unambiguous, decentralized ownership of non-physical assets".[6]

But NFTs are not the only currency floating in the Metaverse. Cryptocurrency which is the generic name for the different and unique forms of trading currency within this parallel commercial cyberspace, also contains within it, Bitcoins. Bitcoins is simply a specific name for currency token, and it was the very first crypto token that was introduced. A formal definition of it would be that,

> "A bitcoin is a decentralised digital currency that operates without a financial system or governmental

authorities. It utilises peer to peer transactions on a digital network that records all digital transactions". (Ibid)

Implicit in this very definition is the fact that there is no (a) governmental authority backing up this and attesting to its authenticity and (b) No single individual or entity on the door of which, default transactions can be laid or attributed to. Naturally, this means that there has to be complete transparency for all transactions and all the peers are joint stakeholders to any transaction which will be digitally stored in at least one known location. This may appear highly risky when there is no any one single individual or authority who can take the onus of blame and it appears on the surface that criminals (cybercriminals) will enjoy borderless trading that exists outside the known financial system, but the amazing fact is that this system works! Money laundering in crypto which was already very low, has gone even lower. Because of the existence of provenance, laundering in crypto is becoming more and more difficult every day. As a result, the percentage of illicit trades in the global crypto community is decreasing from an already low 0.62 percent in 2020 to 0.15 percent in 2021.[7]

Conclusion

The Metaverse, both as a concept and as an application is currently, still very much in an 'embryonic' stage. Thematically, technologically and commercially, although still at a nascent level, it is nevertheless, continually evolving and coalescing with other allied technologies. Most people, especially the senior segment of the population are quite naturally averse and apprehensive about embracing new technologies that are a complete breakaway not only technically but also conceptually based on a praxis that is far ahead of its time. But complete acceptance is just a matter of time as blockchain technology continues to grow, refine and redefine itself with every new iteration and development. NFTs and cryptocurrencies are waiting in the wings to completely replace national and international transactions in the same way that UPI payments are slowly but surely gaining ground over cash payments in our day-to-day transactions. Artificial Intelligence, Machine Learning, Augmented Reality and Virtual Reality, all terms that were at one stage, Greek and Latin to the viewer or reader are now, in the common usage dictionary of even the average computer literate citizen. It is just a matter of time before these new technologies are not only embraced by each and every household, but society cannot even begin to imagine how life possibly existed at one time without these immersive and sophisticated new media.

References

[1] Rohlinger, D. A. (2019). *New media and society*. New York University Press.

[2] Andrew, C. (2022). Metaverse for Beginners: A Guide to Help You Learn About Metaverse, Virtual Reality and Investing in NFTs.

[3] Anderson, J., & Rainie, L. (2022). The Metaverse in 2040. *Pew Research Centre*, *30*

[4] Nevelsteen, K. J. (2018). Virtual world, defined from a technological perspective and applied to video games, mixed reality, and the Metaverse. *Computer animation and virtual worlds*, *29*(1), e1752.

[5] Gaming Market Size, Share & Growth Revenues (2030) (n.d.). Retrieved September 28, 2023 from https://www.fortunebusinessinsights.com/gamingmarket-105730).

[6] Andrew, C. (2022). Metaverse for Beginners: A Guide to Help You Learn About Metaverse, Virtual Reality and Investing in NFTs.

[7] Van Rijmenam, M. (2022). Step into the metaverse: How the immersive internet will unlock a trillion-dollar social economy. John Wiley & Sons.

INDEX

ACORN, 123
affiliate marketing, 5
AI anchors, 8
Alan Toffler, 162
Alan Turing, 140, 152
algorithms, 40, 55, 83, 87, 137, 149, 153, 154, 155, 165
AR/VR technologies, 126
artificial intelligence, 111, 140, 142
Artificial Intelligence, xiv, xix, 87, 91, 136, 140, 148, 158, 176
augmented reality, 92, 124
Augmented Reality, xiv, 92, 124, 125, 134, 150, 171, 176
avatar, vii
Avatar, 160, 169
Backpropagation, 143
big data, 48, 87, 109, 146, 147
Big Data, xix, 41, 55, 78, 144, 146, 147
blockchain, 94, 137, 168, 176
Blockchain, 94, 137, 166
blogs, 50, 82, 118
Blogs, 82
broadcast journalism, 117
Broadcast journalism, 117
citizen journalist, xi, 117, 119, 121, 123, 126, 131, 132, 134

clickbait advertising, 89
clickbait headline, 59, 88, 89, 90
Consultational Interactivity,, 103
consumerism, xviii, 17, 78, 129
Consumerism, xviii, 14, 78
content creation, 4, 5, 7, 13, 136
Conversational Interactivity, 103
cookies, 55, 57, 165
copyright, 22, 24, 25, 27, 28, 29, 31, 32, 34, 35, 36, 39, 166, 173
Copyright, ii, xvii, 22, 23, 24, 25, 26, 27, 29, 33, 34, 35, 37
Copyright Protection Act, xvii, 23, 24, 33
crowd funding, 144
cryptocurrency, 173
Cryptocurrency, 166, 173, 174
cyber bullying, xviii, 57, 58, 77
Cyber bullying, xviii, 58
cyber harassment, 67, 69, 73, 74
Cyber harassment, xviii, 58
cyber pirates, 38
cyber stalking, 64
Cyber stalking, 64, 76

cyber threats, 53, 63
cybercrime, 37, 38, 64, 67, 75
data journalism, 96, 97, 98, 99, 100, 101, 102, 104, 105, 107, 108, 110, 111, 115, 116
Data journalism, 96, 99, 114
data visualisation, 106
Data visualisation, 106
Dataminr, 47, 54
datasets, 53, 101, 153
Datasets, 100
dataveillance, 40, 165
Dataveillance, 40, 44
decentralised environment, 173
Decentralised Environment, 167
deep fakes, 7, 122
Deep Learning, 87
deterrents, 36, 37
Digital Divide, 21
digital marketing, 4, 78, 79, 82, 84, 86, 87, 88, 91, 92, 93, 94, 112
Digital marketing, 80, 91, 94
Digital Rights Management, 28
digital technologies, 3, 6, 7
DMCA, 31, 32
e-commerce, 78, 81
E-commerce, 78, 81
facebook, 51
Facebook, vii, 42, 43, 44, 55, 56, 61, 62, 81, 84, 89, 127, 131, 161, 169
fact checking, 5

fake identities, 62
fake news, 7, 122
Flickr, 41
FORTRAN, 143
globalisation, 9, 10, 11, 12, 16, 17, 18, 78
Globalisation, xvii, 10, 12, 14, 17, 19, 20, 79
Google Analytics,, 88, 112, 164
influencer marketing, 85
Influencer Marketing, xviii, 85
Information Technology Act, 23, 65
Instagram, 62, 81, 84, 93, 103, 127, 129
intellectual property, 21, 22, 24, 25, 26, 27, 29, 33, 34, 173
Intellectual Property, ix, xiii, xvii, 21, 22, 23, 24, 33, 35, 37, 39, 167
Intellectual Property Rights,, xvii, 21, 37
interactivity, 3, 100, 102, 103, 105
Interactivity, 100, 104
IPR, 25
LISP, 141, 142
machine learning, viii, 149, 152, 153, 154
Machine Learning, xv, xix, xx, 87, 91, 136, 137, 152, 156, 176
meta, 163, 172
Meta, vii, 131, 161, 164, 169, 172
metaverse, 167, 169, 177

Metaverse, xx, 137, 159, 160, 161, 162, 163, 164, 165, 166, 167, 168, 169, 170, 172, 173, 174, 175, 177

Metropolis, 159

Minecraft, 171

misinformation, 122, 127

mobile journalism, 118, 121, 122, 126, 127, 129, 134

Mobile journalism, 118, 120

Mojo, 117

NFTs, xx, 137, 166, 173, 174, 176, 177

Non-Fungible Tokens, xx, 173

Paid Search Marketing, 83

Pew Research Centre, 43, 68, 127, 177

piracy, ix, xiii, 21, 23, 24, 25, 26, 28, 29, 30, 32, 35, 36, 37, 39

Piracy, xvii, 21, 27, 29, 32, 39

Registrational Interactivity, 103

reinforced learning, 155

Reinforced learning, 155

Roblox, 171

Search Engine Optimisation, 83, 112

Search Retargeting, 83

Site Remarketing, 83

Snapchat, 41, 93, 146

Snow Crash, 159

supervised learning, 153, 154

Supervised learning, 153

surveillance, 40, 42, 48, 52, 53, 54, 55, 81

Surveillance, 44, 53

Telecom Regulatory Authority of India, 29

Telegram, 63

TRAI, 29, 32

Transmissional interactivity, 103

TRIPS, 23, 24, 38

UGC, 122, 128

user-generated content, 122, 124, 127

virtual reality, ix, 124, 125, 164

Virtual Reality, xiv, 92, 124, 150, 163, 171, 172, 176, 177

VPN, 28, 44

web analytics, 112, 113

Web Analytics, 87, 88, 112

WhatsApp, 63

Wikileaks, 97, 98

World Intellectual Property Organisation, 24

XML (Extensible Markup Language), 145

Youtube, 31, 57, 131

www.ingramcontent.com/pod-product-compliance
Lightning Source LLC
LaVergne TN
LVHW041708070526
838199LV00045B/1256